Out of the Frying Pan, Into the Fire

Out of the Frying Pan Into the Fire

The Restless Journey of Marianne "Jolly" Robinson

REGENT PRESS
BERKELEY, CALIFORNIA

Copyright © 2010 by Marianne Robinson

ISBN 13: 978-1-58790-206-2
ISBN 10: 1-58790-206-0
Library of Congress Catalog Number: 2010928111

This autobiography is based on personal memories, materials from my archives, and research in the process of writing. I take full responsibility for its contents.

Cover art by Tom Schultz

Printed by InkWorks Press 147
Berkeley, California

Published by
REGENT PRESS
www.regentpress.net
regentpress@mindspring.com

✿ ✿ ✿

Other books by Marianne Robinson

Poetry
SPIDERWEBS AND RAINBOWS
PIECES TOGETHER
YESTERDAY AND TODAY
AWAKE AT 2 A.M.
POEMS FOR VICKI

Poems and Prose
BECOMING IS ALL

Dedication

To my parents and extended family of freethinkers
who planted the seeds that sprouted and bore fruit
as I sought my way through life.

To wise educators who said, "Learn by doing, by exploring,
by asking questions and acting on your values."

To the unsung women and men whose lives touched mine
and taught me more than the experts.

To Bill Robinson, father of my only child,
whose soul was deep, whose artistry wide.

To my beloved one and only, Vicki Sue Robinson, whose life of
music and theater, joy and sorrow, was much too short.

And to Tom Schultz, my loving and loyal partner of 40+ years,
whose paintings, humor, and caring brighten the lives of many people.

Preface

Among the formative experiences of my childhood and adolescence were an extended family and community of freethinkers, two unforgettable years in a small school that focused on "learning by doing," and many moves during the Great Depression and World War II. While I heard early recordings and sang songs of protest against fascism abroad, I witnessed race and class discrimination close to home. All those experiences formed the frying pan from which I leaped into the fire after high school.

My adult life has been a juggling act of jobs, singing, activism in labor, anti-war, and women's movements, motherhood and single parenting, poetry, college courses, photography, teaching, research, self-employment (and unemployment), and creative projects. My daughter's shining spirit after her death at 45 pulled at my heartstrings daily as I wrote this book.

The determination to make personal choices in the face of relentless economic necessity is a central theme in my life story. It is familiar to those who juggle jobs, single parenting, activism, and creative pursuits in their pursuit of meaning and fulfillment in a society focused on college, career, and above all, upward mobility—"the race to the top."

A few poems are woven into this story. Some "wrote themselves" as immediate expression of the life I was living; others were written years afterwards as I looked back. The illustrations that follow each chapter are part of my personal collection.

Introduction

Marianne "Jolly" Robinson has led a rich and eventful life spanning eight decades, during which she knew prominent people and participated in momentous events. Her story gives fascinating insights into family complexities, intentional communities, folk and topical music, labor and women's movements, struggles for economic and racial justice, and much more. Her experiences were certainly unique, yet they connected with the lives of ordinary people, particularly working mothers struggling to survive and raise children.

Born into a family with nontraditional views on religion, education, and lifestyle, Marianne describes the experimental school and intentional community that also shaped her childhood and adolescence. She heard and sang folk and topical songs in the 1940s, and folk music remained a vital part of her life. In 1948 she worked for People's Songs with Pete Seeger, Woody Guthrie, and other folk singers/songwriters, and sang in the Presidential campaign of Henry Wallace and the Progressive Party. Traveling in the Midwest with a Union Caravan in 1949 was another unforgettable experience. She went on to work with labor unions as an employee, singer/organizer, photographer, and teacher of Labor Songs as History.

While many musicians and actors experienced the worst of the anti-communist Red Scare of the 1950s, she struggled through the decade as a wife and mother, singer and Communist Party member. During the 1960s upsurge in folk music she worked for Albert Grossman, manager of Bob Dylan and Peter, Paul and Mary, then for folklorist Alan Lomax, who convinced her to enroll in Margaret Mead's anthropology courses at Columbia University. She began writing poetry in 1964 when her daughter, Vicki Sue, was 10.

During the 1970s, she developed a strong interest in photography and worked as a freelance photojournalist for labor and women's organizations. While working for

Gloria Steinem at *Ms.* Magazine, she got a foundation grant to conduct an independent research study on adult low-income women going to college while raising children. Also in the 70s, she edited an audio/video trade magazine and then became Administrator of a new Occupational Safety And Health Program for a large public sector union. Meanwhile, Vicki Sue Robinson had launched a successful career as a singer and recording artist.

In 1980 Marianne and her partner, Tom Schultz, moved to Berkeley, California, where she has lived and worked at various jobs and creative projects, with her daughter and her mother ever-present in her thoughts and her writings. Her story is stitched together with poems, photos, and illustrations, giving it much substance.

Marianne Robinson's story is vivid testimony to the contributions of countless little-known individuals who have found ways to make life better for all, an inspiration to future generations. In the midst of difficult personal survival can come a creative, lifelong commitment to social justice, human rights, and peace.

> Ronald D. Cohen, author of *Rainbow Quest: The Folk Music Revival and American Society,* and *Work and Sing: A History of Occupational and Labor Union Songs in the United States.*

Contents

PROLOGUE

CHAPTER ONE
The Crucible
1

CHAPTER TWO
You Don't Learn This in College
27

CHAPTER THREE
Moves, Marriage, and Motherhood
49

CHAPTER FOUR
Expanding Vistas, New Challenges
72

CHAPTER FIVE
Starting Again in New Terrain
105

CHAPTER SIX
Change and Loss
135

CHAPTER SEVEN
Into the 21st Century
162

EPILOGUE
171

Prologue

From her window seat on the airplane, she watched the wooded hills of Pennsylvania slowly shifting far below. This was her first time on an airplane, and it felt surreal to be suspended high above the earth between two unfamiliar places—the one she had just left and the one she was headed to. In her 20 years, she had never traveled alone to meet strangers in a strange town. "This must be happening to someone else," she thought. "Yesterday I had no idea I would be flying from Providence to Pittsburgh after rehearsing for weeks in New York."

The plan had been to work with local leaders in the Progressive Party campaign to elect Henry Wallace as President in 1948. Her Caravan, one of several performing troupes around the country, had driven to Providence, Rhode Island from Manhattan—seven people packed into a car towing a trailer full of luggage. Next morning, as guests in the home of a campaigner, the troupe was mapping out its schedule at breakfast when an urgent phone call came from campaign headquarters. Seems the musician who accompanied the Caravan in Pittsburgh, Pennsylvania had taken ill and they needed someone to replace him right away. Within an hour she was on her way to join a performing troupe she did not know and had not rehearsed with.

As she pondered the rapid chain of events that had brought her to this place, the plane was coming in for a landing, and in minutes she would meet the people who would take her to the beginning of another adventure.

This unexpected flight to a new adventure is but a tiny episode in the real-life story chronicled in the chapters that follow.

CHAPTER ONE
The Crucible

As she was giving birth to me on the Fourth of July, my mother could hear kids playing in the water gushing from open hydrants in the street. It was Independence Day in Philadelphia, Pennsylvania, "the birthplace of liberty." The year was 1928. The official name on the birth certificate was Marianne, but my mother preferred "Jolly," and Jolly was the name I was known by.

My brother Jac arrived two years later, in June 1930. The story is that his name, Jacquin, was taken from a billboard advertising brandy, but he was called Jac or Jackie, and few people knew his given name or the story behind it. In this and many other ways, our family and friends observed or created customs in nontraditional ways.*

My mother, Amy Lou Potter, had English and French Canadian ancestors. My father, Henry Smolens, was a Jew whose father had emigrated to Philadelphia from Ukraine in the 1890s. Neither parent was religious in any formal sense. They were freethinkers, agnostics, nonbelievers in religious dogma.

Henry first visited the village of Arden, Delaware in 1917 with a friend from Philadelphia who had a summer cottage there. Amy, her brother Lloyd, and their parents, Cora and Ed Potter, were year-round dwellers in Arden at that time. Henry, at 20, had fallen in love with Amy when she was 13, but her parents insisted they wait to marry till she was 20. During most of the intervening years, the Potter family lived in Fairhope, Alabama, a similar small community.

Amy was a talented artist. She had attended The School of Industrial Arts in Philadelphia (now Pennsylvania Academy of Fine Art). Though she loved painting and drawing and took it seriously, she did not care for the requirements of "higher education" and spent more time sketching outside of

---

* Jac and I called everyone—relatives and friends of all ages—by their first names. We called our mother Amy, our father Henry, grandparents Cora and Eddie, uncles and aunts Fan and Joe, Mike and Bertha, and so on. My parents' friends were Gladys and Bill, Pat and Cy, Hilary and Bud, Miriam, Danny. No one was "Mrs. This or Mr. That" unless they were not in the extended family.

school than in formal classes. When she and Henry married, she gave up art as a profession. Though Henry may have influenced her decision, her friends and family were disappointed when she turned down a scholarship to the Academy.

Henry Smolens was a salesman, in and out of work during the Great Depression, first in retail stores, then for Mack Trucks and General Tires. He turned to real estate sales, and became a realtor with his own company in the housing boom during World War II. As the youngest of five children, and the first to be born in this country, Henry had known poverty and hunger in his childhood and blamed his father, who lost jobs because of his beliefs as a "radical anarchist." He was determined he was going to make a good living, have food on the table, and provide for his family.

We lived in several places during my early childhood while Henry worked or looked for work in those Depression years. From Philadelphia, we moved to Arden, to Washington DC to live with Amy's parents, then two suburban communities near Philadelphia, and back to Arden once more. Arden was my home for eight years before, during, and just after World War II.

Pre-school

My first vivid memories are of Penn Wynne, a suburb of Philadelphia, where we moved when I was about four. We lived in a semi-detached row house with a small front yard, a willow tree, and concrete steps leading up to the front door. I went to kindergarten in a public school. The room with little desks and chairs was hardly memorable, except (for me) the time a kid threw up in a waste-basket. In my eagerness to read, I walked from our house to the nearby public library and brought home books. I'd sit on the sofa and read aloud, asking what this word meant and how that word was pronounced. Once I went to Sunday School with a friend, and afterwards my mother asked what we did. I told her we colored pictures of Jesus and sang "Hey, Nonny, Nonny and a Ha Cha-Cha!" I have a mental picture of chairs stacked in a church basement. Jac and I did a lot of drawing and painting with Amy's constant encouragement—coloring books were forbidden and I didn't see one till much later.

Aunt Fan (Henry's sister), her husband Joe and daughter Phyllis, lived with us at Penn Wynne. Their son Schuyler had broken his neck in a fatal diving accident, and they were devastated. They lived with us at a time of personal tragedy and Depression-era insecurity.

During a thunderstorm, Amy sat on the bed next to the window with Jac and me. I said the thunder sounded "like God throwing pianos down the stairs." She explained that we could tell how far off the lightning was by counting the seconds after a big flash before the awesome thunder clap: "One, two, three, four—CRA-A-A-CK!"

We had a Victrola—floor model radio/phonograph—and lots of 78rpm records, and we learned songs by singing along with Vernon Dalhart and other crooners of the 30s. I remember tunes and a few words from "Barnacle Bill, the Sailor," "An Old Man's Story," "Sinking of the Vestris," "Abdul, Abulbul, Amir." On a family car trip, we stopped at a tavern and entered through the Ladies' Entrance at the side. Someone put a nickel in the jukebox, and I remember "Let's All Sing Like the Birdies Sing." It's the first song I recall hearing away from home. The year was 1933.

Robin Hill

When I was six, we moved from Penn Wynne to a rented cottage at Robin Hill, a Philadelphia suburb one mile outside Media, Pennsylvania,. It was a picturesque place, with bay windows, pleasant living space, and a second floor for play, overnight guests, and storage. There were six other houses on the hill and a few other children. A winding dirt road led from the main road up to our house at the top of the hill. Jac and I waited at the bottom of the hill for Henry to come home from work and gleefully stood on the running board all the way home!

The lawn sloped downhill in front of the cottage, the woods were uphill behind the house, and a big field across the fence was filled with tall weeds and flowers. Amy took a photograph of me sitting on that fence in the fairy costume she made—complete with gossamer wings, one of many costumes she kept in a big chest in the attic. In another photograph I was dressed as a Dutch girl, looking at the tulips and tall hollyhocks in front of the house. Her water color painting of me as a gypsy occupies a place on my wall with other family pictures.

We kids tied tall grasses together to make huts, where we hid from grown-ups and made up games. In the woods behind our house a big, rotting tree stump became "the stump of Shanghai," a mythical spot for young boys' games, and a deep hole below the stump went "all the way to China." One time Jackie, as we called him, sold lemonade near the dirt road approaching our house. His hand-lettered sign read "POOT MONEY IN BOX."

At the bottom of our hill two roads intersected at a bridge where Rose Tree Road crossed Ridley Creek, with farm fields on the other side. Sometimes Amy took us on picnics along the creek bank. When the creek rose and threatened to flood the small bridge, a highway patrolman directed traffic at the intersection. Jac and I were thrilled when Ollie would let us direct traffic under his supervision. The creek and its marshy banks were the scene of a terrifying nightmare I had about walking up a black metal ramp toward a huge, windowless black wagon to the solemn warlike beat of drums, as if marching to an execution. We had just seen the movie, "The Last of the Mohicans," a classic of the 30s.

Mealtime gatherings of family and friends around the big oak table in the small dining room were wonderful socializing experiences, sometimes three generations sharing conversation, animated discussion of current events, word games, drawing games, and always laughter. Frequent guests were Florence "Reds" Taylor and Albert V. Dreher ("Dreary"), Amy's friends from art school, as vivid as yesterday in my mind's eye. I practiced piano lessons in a small, windowed room off the living room, where Uncle Lloyd slept when he stayed with us. I can still see the four-poster bed under the window in my bedroom, where the hill sloped up to the woods. In that bedroom a glamorous, blue-skirted dressing table with three-way mirror mysteriously appeared one Christmas morning, complete with an elegant, square blue glass clock with a star in each corner.

Some of my memories of those years have been kept alive by the tiny, part-handwritten, part-typed booklet that Amy kept of conversations and descriptions by her children she recorded over an eight-year period from 1932, when Jac was two and I was four. It remains a one-of-a-kind, authentic record of her children's personalities, experiences, and family relationships. Her hand-lettered title is "The Jackie & Jolly Book." It is my most treasured possession, something Amy did that I've never seen in another family. It's a tangible illustration of the way that she valued free expression and enjoyed her children's development. It's far more revealing than photographs; it captures our words and phrases and opens a window into what was going on in our minds, our relationships, our observations of the world as we grew up.

The School in Rose Valley

For me, the best experience of the Robin Hill years was attending The School in Rose Valley for two of those years. The small experimental school was built and run by parents and teachers, combining the "learn by doing" ideas of John Dewey with "organic education," the progressive learning theories and practices embraced by its founders. With no academic credentials, Amy was able to teach art there for two years, making our half-tuition possible. Uncle Lloyd, who lived with us for a time, taught wood shop at the school. Rose Valley practiced education in the best sense, encouraging

The School in Rose Valley

The School in Rose Valley was patterned on the *School for Organic Education*, founded in 1907 by educator Marietta Johnson in Fairhope, Louisiana. It is praised in John Dewey's influential book Schools of Tomorrow (1915). Dewey and Johnson were founding members of the *Progressive Education Association*. In 2009, The School in Rose Valley states its mission and core values as follows:

Mission
The School in Rose Valley is a progressive school for children in preschool through sixth grade. In our classrooms and our wooded campus, teachers and students create experiences that arouse curiosity, stretch muscles, strengthen initiative, and stimulate questions. We guide children to know themselves, to delight in learning, and to understand their opportunities and responsibilities in our community and the world.

Core values
The School in Rose Valley respects childhood and values democracy, diversity, and sustainability. Children's perspectives and needs inform all aspects of our school. We believe that children should develop balance in body and mind through intensive classroom study, quiet time, vigorous play, experiences of the natural world, and reflection on our role as its stewards. At The School in Rose Valley, democracy encompasses freedom, responsibility, and participation. Our students become competent and active citizens by fulfilling real responsibilities, from tending our campus to partnering with other communities in learning and service. We honor diversity, appreciate difference, and value respectful communication. We explore the complexity of natural and social ecosystems, advancing sustainability as a personal, campus, local, and global practice.

Source: http://www.theschoolinrosevalley.org/

children to explore in a hands-on way rather than focusing on formal classes, tests, and grades. Teachers and parents were dedicated to educating the whole child. To instill a love of learning was the guiding principle.

The school's several small buildings, constructed by parents and teachers, were in a rural setting, reached by a dirt road off the main road, with fields and trees and a creek nearby, as well as scattered houses. Field trips were part of our schooling. After a trip to the local observatory, I became absorbed in astronomy with my eight-year-old friend Christy. We made a frieze of the solar system around the wall in the classroom. Another trip was to the Scott Paper factory in the nearby industrial town of Chester. In science classes we illustrated the evolution of life on earth around the classroom at a time when the theory was widely controversial in science, government, and education.

Each day began with an informal circle of chairs in which we were encouraged to talk about what was on our minds. We went on nature walks right near the school, bringing back insects for science class, and I remember dissecting a small mammal. We had good lunches, and naps on cots for the younger kids. There was basic sex education from a book written for children. There was no separation of girls and boys—we all wore overalls and played soccer and climbed trees and fed the goats and chickens. Boys and girls both did hands-on wood shop. I made a footstool and a birdhouse.

There were no tests, grades, or report cards. Children were grouped by ages—6s and 7s, 8s and 9s, 10s and 11s. It was considered important that children learn to integrate their social and physical skills within their age group. There were no As or Fs; instead, brief typed reports written by the teachers were compiled, typed, and mailed to parents at the end of each half year, summarizing observed strengths as well as areas that needed improvement. I still have copies of mine, which Amy gave me years later.

At the end of the second year at Rose Valley, our family income would not permit our parents to continue sending us there. State regulations had changed, and teachers were required to have academic credentials. Thus Amy, a fine artist with art school education but no degree, was disqualified. Another factor was the Depression, which continued until the U.S. entry into World War II ended it.

From the Rose Valley experience, at eight I was transplanted to Sandy Bank public elementary school in nearby Media. It felt like being sent to prison—an institutional setting with rows of desks, rules, and discipline, bells ringing to designate the end and beginning of each class, of recess or lunch or the end of the school day. I entered the 4th grade and had my first encounter with tests, grades, and report cards.

At Sandy Bank I had my first experience with anti-Semitism when a boy sitting behind me called me a "pork dodger" (the only time I ever heard that term). As some of the kids snickered, I stood up and declared proudly that my father happened to be Jewish. To my relief, the teacher was supportive and told the class that name-calling was not appropriate behavior. The boys played rough in the school yard, and girls were treated with derision and lack of respect. So, besides previously unknown regimentation, that public school introduced me to sexism and anti-Semitism.

Early influences

At Robin Hill, besides the gatherings with friends and family, we would listen to FDR's fireside chats in front of the radio in the living room, and enjoy the popular radio dramas and comedians of the 30s. At Christmas grandparents Cora and Eddie would visit, and we'd take turns opening our presents around the tree on Christmas morning. One year my grand-mother made me a big doll house and all the furniture, curtains, and dolls to go with it. It occupied a table by the window in the second-floor attic room, where I made up stories about its occupants.

Outdoors we played in the woods and meadows and experienced nature firsthand. There was a good balance between social and intellectual life and daily connection with the natural world. Amy loved gardening, especially growing flowers. Her mother, Cora, was a gardener who had been part of a cooperative farm called Llano, in Louisiana. The Potters—Cora, Ed, Lloyd and Amy—had lived in Fairhope, Alabama, a small Single Tax colony with a School of Organic Education that became the model for the School in Rose Valley. Intentional communities, experimental education, and cooperative living were strong influences in the Potter family and in my formative years.

Henry's family history, though mostly unknown to me, was nontraditional in other ways. His father, Ozer Smolenskin, was a scholar, writer and teacher; a learned man, mostly self-taught. He had left rabbinical studies in Ukraine at 13 when he was caught reading "outside the Torah" secular books in Polish, Russian, and other languages. Disowned by his grandmother who supported his Hebrew studies by selling ribbons and handkerchiefs, he became a heretic, a visionary, a freethinker and anarchist. He loved humanity and felt (and wrote) passionately against injustice in any form. Having emigrated to the U.S. with his family in the 1890s, he was accused of being an anarchist conspirator after President McKinley's assassination in 1901.

Family values

I grew up with little fear of authority. On the mantel over the fireplace in the Arden house were the words, in Old English lettering: "WE SAY OR KEEP STILL AT OUR OWN SWEET WILL." I felt supported to be outspoken, without fear of censorship. I was definitely not taught to be seen and not heard. I never got that message at home, with my parents' friends, or at the School in Rose Valley. Polite, yes, respect for others and their views, but not being silent because I was a child. This did not mean that children didn't have to go to bed earlier or that we could do whatever we wanted, but that within the limits of our physical, mental, and emotional age, we were treated as equals and encouraged to express ourselves, to learn and experiment, question and explore.

My brother and I were quite different in most ways, though we shared a delight in nature and the outdoors, music and art. In many ways I see Jac as being more like Amy and me as more like Henry. And that was played out—Jac is a rural person and I became an urban dweller, drawn to the city and its opportunities for intellectual growth and development, and political activism. Jac's growth and aptitudes led him to art and working with his hands, much like Amy. He is an artist and wood sculptor with a deep connection to organic, natural subjects and forms. He's quieter, less verbal and more inward, in contrast to Jolly, the extrovert, who's more people-oriented, exploring the wider world. Jac is happy to live in the rural Eastern Shore of Maryland. He lived in other places but never went too far from his roots, while I kept reaching out, going farther afield, seeking new experiences.

Amy's first child, Alan, had died soon after his birth (of jaundice, they said), but I didn't learn that for many years. I came along next, and almost didn't make it. Amy had been a vegetarian of strong moral persuasion. When I wasn't gaining weight after a few weeks, Henry took her to a doctor, who ordered her to eat meat and dairy and fatty foods and told her to change her diet if she wanted her daughter to live. By the time Jac came along, she was no longer a vegetarian. Though he had more illnesses growing up than I did, he turned out to be hardier in the long run. My sensitivities and allergies were more related to Henry's genes (and, I concluded later, to Amy's nutritional deficiencies before I was born).

Between Jac and me there were the usual tensions of siblings two years apart, but we got along pretty well. We had friends at Robin Hill and in Rose Valley School. There were family gatherings with an extended family of relatives and friends, and a supportive environment. At Robin Hill there were meadows and places to play and make up kids' fantasies and stories. Amy's costume chest was a source of imaginative play, there were paints and crayons and paper and no lack of encouragement to use them. She was a full-time mother, and when she taught art at the school we attended, she was nearby. There were trips by car to Arden and to visit the grandparents in Washington, and we would play games in the car. One game was to see who could spot the most out-of-state license plates. "Beaver" was our favorite. As we'd come to a curve in the road, there'd be an S-shaped sign, and whoever spotted it first would yell "Beaver!" and chalk up a point.

The Scopes Trial

The Scopes Trial (often called the Scopes Monkey Trial) was a highly publicized American court case in 1925 that tested a Tennessee law, the Butler Act, which forbade the teaching of any theory of evolution in any state-funded educational establishment. Brought about when the American Civil Liberties Union (ACLU) encouraged John T. Scopes to stand trial for teaching a high school science course that included evolution in the textbook, the court became a stage for the dramatic confrontation between fundamentalist Christian William Jennings Bryan and liberal Clarence Darrow (the latter representing teacher John T. Scopes). Although media attention was focused on the trial, and it has remained famous in popular culture, the case did not resolve any issues, even on appeal. Forty-three years later, the U.S. Supreme Courtdetermined that statutes banning the teaching of evolution were unconstitutional, a year after the Butler Act had been repealed. By the end of the 20th century, many local school districts required the teaching of evolution, and theories of creationism and intelligent design were banned. At the heart of the question raised in the Scopes trial is the issue of the separation of church and state, or government control over the role of religion in American public life. Unless all people can agree on universal principles, which can then be embodied in law, issues of what state-funded education must and must not teach the children cannot be finally resolved.

Source: New World Encyclopedia, http://www.newworldencyclopedia.org/entryScopesTrial

While Amy may have felt embarrassed by my precociousness as a young child, she worried more about Jac. When, as a teen-aged boy, he got into trouble during the week, Amy had to answer to our father when he came home on Friday from his work in Philadelphia. Mother and son were both fearful of Henry's authoritarian anger. I learned early on to avoid punishment by being "a good girl."

Depression years

During the early Depression years, we lived with Amy's parents (Cora and Ed) in Friendship Heights, near Washington. Ed Potter had been a journalist but at that time he worked for the American Tuberculosis Association. I was aware that he was quite the dapper ladies' man who would drive women in his Chevrolet to meetings or charity fundraisers. He was a good-natured, fun-loving man, while my grandmother Cora was the hard-nosed, practical business person in the family. One story has Ed telling Cora that another of his business ventures had fallen through. He shrugged philosophically, "Oh well, chalk it up to profit and loss." To which Cora replied in exasperation, "Can you tell me where the profit is?"

Henry told of visiting sessions of Congress and walking through the halls with only a dime in his pocket, the tantalizing smell of food coming from the dining room. He heard Congress-men talking about the big issues of the day—the New Deal, with its government programs to provide relief and rescue the economy. One larger-than-life character was Senator Huey Long, Louisiana Democrat and passionate social reformer. Another topic of lively conversation was the Scopes "Monkey" Trial and the unresolved question of whether evolution could be taught in U.S. schools.

And of course there was animated conversation about the rise of Nazi Germany, and the looming prospect of a second World War.

When friends and relatives would come, we played drawing games like "Head, Body & Legs," and oral word games and riddles, part of the family lore. I learned a lot of my language skills at home. I would try out words that I had read in a book, and when I used them in the wrong place, the grown-ups would laugh, or correct me. But I kept on trying them out.

Grandparents—freethinkers all

Sadly, I didn't see or know much of my Jewish grandfather, whom we called Oscar, and his wife Sophie. Henry was Oscar's fifth child, the first to be born in the United States. Henry brought him to visit us in Arden shortly before he died. I remember Oscar as sweet, loving, and kind; a small man, maybe 5'5". There had been an estrangement between father and son. Henry had gone hungry as a child when Oscar had trouble keeping jobs because of his political views, and because he disliked selling houses and insurance to poor, struggling folks. Oscar, the educated scholar and teacher, didn't last at the jobs he did get, and writing tracts for the Anarchist cause didn't help. In the introduction to his book, he describes losing a job at a pharmacy.

"From 1897 to 1901 I worked very hard in a pharmacy in Philadelphia. At work I met some good American men and began to study psychology. They used to call me 'the white collar man' and I was quite friendly with the other white collar men. I proselytized to them, wrote brochures and papers and felt very happy, although I wasn't making a good salary.

"All of a sudden some crazy 'Polack' came along and killed the President

[McKinley]. Then began a terrible inquisition. It was like a crazy house. They arrested people and accused everyone, and I was frightened because I had been outspoken and had written propaganda. They passed repressive laws against radicals and anarchists and tried to enforce them. Although I was an American citizen, suddenly I felt I had a lot of enemies and I was looked at with suspicion, as though I were poison.

"One day I came to work to find my work pants torn and my shoes nailed to the floor. When I reported this to my boss, who had been a good friend, he said, 'I'm sorry, Oscar, but I cannot help you. The world is crazy now and I think you'd better resign.'"

On Amy's side things were quite different. Her parents were strongly influential in my life. Her father, Edwin Stanton Potter, was of English origin going back generations, and had become a church-going Unitarian at some point, like his mother. When he lived with us in Arden in his elder years, he went to "meetings" at a Unitarian church in Wilmington, and I was surprised because I had thought he was not a churchgoer. My grandmother was Cora Louise Lightbown—the last name taken by her father when he stowed away on a ship from England. Cora's mother was partly French Canadian and, the story goes, partly Native American.

Cora and Ed had participated in several intentional and cooperative colonies from the late 19th through the first half of the 20th century. One was Helicon Home Colony in Englewood, New Jersey, across the Hudson River from New York City. Upton Sinclair, who also lived in Arden for a time, had been instrumental in its founding, but it was destined to last only a year. When Amy was two years old, the building the Potter family lived in was destroyed by a fire of mysterious origin. She told of being lowered by rope from a second story window as the fire engulfed their residence.

Another experimental colony was New Llano, in rural Louisiana, established in 1917 by socialists from California who purchased land and attracted farmers and workers to the cooperative experiment. Deeply inherent in Llano was respect for labor as the source of all value, as in other cooperative communities. It was also one of the first groups in America to adopt the Montessori teaching method at its kindergarten. Commonwealth College, where my Uncle Lloyd went for a time, was based at Llano until it relocated in Mena, Arkansas.

Though I had only a smattering of this history when I was a child, I heard much about Fairhope, Alabama, a Single Tax colony on Mobile Bay where Amy spent some of her youth. Fairhope pioneered in "Organic Education" under the leadership of Marietta Johnson, a dedicated educator who had come from Iowa. The School in Rose Valley had it roots in the same educational theories, derived from John Dewey, Sigmund Freud, and educational innovators of the time.

There had been Catholicism on Cora's side, but she had separated herself from any formal religion or dogma. I had a great time when I went to visit the grandparents in Washington. My brother stayed home with Amy, and I would get on the train at ages 6 and 7 and 8 and chat with grown-ups from my parlor car swivel chair! Arrangements were made with Traveler's Aid to look after me on the trip until I was met by relatives. When the train arrived at Union Station I was turned over to my happy grandparents.

Ed Potter took me on rides around the city in his car—just Eddie and me. He enjoyed it immensely, showing me all the sights and wonders of the nation's capitol. As he drove around DuPont Circle he would chant gleefully, "Now we're cutting the pie crust!" Cora and Ed would take me to the Potomac Basin to see the cherry blossoms starting to bloom at Easter time. And we climbed aboard the underground monorail car that took Congressmen (no women then) from the House to the Senate.

Cora would take me to Woodward & Lothrop, the big department store, and buy me an Easter outfit—everything from a hat to black patent leather shoes, a skirt and blouse—an annual ritual to dress up her granddaughter. Later I learned that Amy had been considered a tomboy in her rejection of the feminine clothing of the day, and when I was born, two years earlier after her firstborn, a boy, had died, she told her mother that she now had a child Cora could dress like a girl.

Once when I went to visit the grandparents in Washington, Cora took me to the massive, awesome Episcopal Cathedral, all dressed up in my Easter bonnet! I could tell there was an affinity there, that she missed something about the imposing structure and ceremony of religion, that she loved the grandeur and rituals of going to church. And of course I was awestruck by the experience.

Their address then (mid-to-late 1930s) was 3552 "Eye" (I) Street NW. The house was a typical Washington brownstone, front steps, a back yard and an alley that ran behind the rows of houses. Cora grew squash, tomatoes, string beans and cucumbers in the backyard garden. I can still hear the strawberry vendor as he pushed his cart down the alley crying, "Stra-a-awber-ries, 10 cents a quart!" It was a two-story house, with living room, dining room, and kitchen downstairs and three bedrooms on the second floor. After Ed played

The Village of Arden

Sculptor Frank Stephens and architect Will Price believed in both Henry George's Single Tax philosophy and William Morris's Arts and Crafts principles. The Single Tax movement in the U.S. believed that the best way to raise government money was by a single tax on land only, whether the land was improved or not. William Morris, an Englishman, rebelled against modern cities and industry and advocated a return to craft production, good design, and village life.

Stephens and Price first came to Delaware in 1895-1896, during the single tax campaign to win political control of the state. The Single Taxers hoped that by gaining control of a small political entity they could put their principles into action and show that they could really work. The campaign failed and many of the activists were jailed, but Price and Stephens did not give up their dream.

In 1900, they purchased a farm in northern New Castle County, Delaware. Price designed a town plan that preserved communal open space and encouraged people to mingle with their neighbors. Stephens and Price adopted "You are welcome hither" as the community motto because they wanted Arden to be a place open to people of all economic levels and political views—a departure in an era when restrictions were the norm. Price never lived in Arden, but Frank Stephens did. His enthusiasm, leadership, and ideas guided Arden from a dream to reality. His son Donald also played a vital role in the community.

Land in Arden was not sold but leased for 99 years. People were free to improve their leaseholds as they chose—the land rent/tax would not increase because of improvements. At first, Arden was a summer community where people lived the simple life in tents or rustic dwellings. After 1905, residents gradually built permanent homes. By 1909, all the land had been leased. There were 115 leaseholders but only 50 year-round residents.

The founding of the Arden Club in 1908 provided an organizational core for community activity. Interest groups and task groups were called gilds rather than committees. From the beginning, Shakespeare's plays were produced in the outdoor Field Theater. Fairs, pageants, and Arden holidays filled the calendar. Monthly town meetings of all the "Ardenfolk" gave everyone— including women and children—a voice and vote in town affairs.

Source: Delaware Historic Society, Wilmington DE, http://www.hsd.org/Lib_ArdenExhibit.htm

and sang at the upright piano, we ate in the dining room at a large table, which I set with Cora's silverware and apple-green dishes. Her home-canned pears were a special treat, sometimes served on lettuce as a salad, sometimes for dessert. The dining room window looked out on the house next door.

When I came down with measles on one visit, the first thing Cora did was to give me an enema, part of her health regimen. When she would feel under the weather, she'd say, "I've broken nature's laws," and she would fast for several days as part of the cleansing ritual. She took me to lectures by natural health gurus of the day. I remember going to hear a food faddist in a big hall. He advised against food combining—no fruits with vegetables, grains with meat, raw with cooked, believing it created problems with digestion and assimilation. This principle surfaced again when I began seeing holistic health practitioners in my 50s.

Cora and Ed came to live with us years later in Arden, in the house they had bought years before. Their presence was stabilizing for me during the war years when Henry worked in Philadelphia and came home only on weekends. It was like having another set of parents—reassuring and loving, an extended family.

Arden

We moved from Robin Hill to Arden in April 1939, when I was nearly 11. The Potter house became available to us, but a bigger reason for moving there was that Amy felt isolated at Robin Hill. Henry went to work every day in the car, and she had no close friends nearby. In Arden there was a real community, where she felt at home. They decided it would be good for all of us to move from an isolated place where we could not afford the progressive school, to Arden, which had a lot to offer kids and parents. Amy could have a social life there in a place she had known since childhood, and some of the original founders and settlers were still there. I finished the 5th grade in the two-room schoolhouse that was "a hop, skip, and a jump" from our new home.

The big, two-story house (plus basement and attic) was on a quarter acre of land at the edge of Sherwood Forest, the woods on Arden's south side that separated the village from neighboring land. Built of stone and wood and stucco, the house featured a sloping roof, front porch the width of the house, and side and back entrances. The big living room had a generous stone fireplace at one end and a bay window at the other. It was spacious enough for a ping pong table and, when furniture was pushed back, for dancing on the hardwood floor! The dining room, scene of countless festive meals, featured the big oak table and upright piano. The kitchen looked out on the woods and an enclosed back porch served as laundry room. There were four bedrooms on the second floor, and one bathroom.

The unfinished attic was storeroom for belongings—and the magical costume chest kept supplied by Amy. The cellar housed the coal furnace that supplied heat and hot water. The yard was part lawn and part vegetable and flower garden, with several apple trees. A tall hedge shielded the front yard from Sherwood Road, which skirted the school yard opposite our house. The dirt driveway led to a one-car garage at the edge of the woods. (It would be many years before anyone had two cars.)

Arden was co-founded in 1900 by Frank Stephens, actor and poet, and Will Price, architect, who together purchased a mile-square tract in northern Delaware seven miles from Wilmington. Like Fairhope, Alabama, it was based on Henry George's Single Tax theory of land held in trust by leaseholders, rather than real estate to be bought and sold. William Morris, craftsman and socialist, was another profound influence on the culture and politics of Arden's founders. Patterned on an English village, there were several large commons set aside for public use, and two outdoor theaters devoted to Shakespearean plays. Frank Stephens's book, *Some Songs,* published by the Arden Press, included "The Arden Song," the beloved anthem sung at community gatherings.

The Arden Song
Words by Frank Stephens (1909)

When crickets sing and kine are homing,
And lanterned stars come seek the sun,
The village lights aslant the gloaming
Come twinkling, twinkling one by one.

Oh, night and sunset glow and starry splendor
And cloud-wreathed eve beneath thy silvery crown,
Ye give to me no guide so true and tender
As are the lights of Arden Town.

When days are drear and ways are weary,
And sad at heart we wanderers roam,
Light, tiny town, thy beacons cheery,
Oh, whispering woodlands call us home.

For stars will shine again and days will brighten,
And rough roads smooth that love shall tread adown,
And evensong ring brave and sad hearts lighten,
As hope leads home to Arden Town.

Arden attracted socialists, anarchists, freethinkers, writers, artists, and theater people. Upton Sinclair, socialist and author of *The Jungle*, Ella Reeve ("Mother") Bloor, socialist and founder of the Communist Party of America, and other notables, lived in Arden for periods.

The Village of Arden had set up a guild system ("gild" in Arden) representing different interests—gardeners, crafts, library, scholars, folk (dance and music) and others. The Gild Hall was a big, two-story barn that had been converted to serve as the community center. Dances, concerts, theater productions, and town meetings were held in the big hall. The Library and Gardeners Gilds occupied rooms at the front of the Hall facing on the road, and there were rest rooms and a dressing room for theater productions. Downstairs there was a kitchen and dining room where weekly community suppers were hosted by various community members. You took your tray, stood in line and got your home-style supper for $1. Meetings were held at the lower level, too, where once there had been a stable.

The town was entirely residential except for one or two small stores and a gas station on the "main road" at the edge of town. The tiny Co-op store, an early consumer cooperative, faced the Arden Green, and the Woolerys had a mom and pop grocery store on another road. The Craft Shop and the Weave Shop housed studios where artists lived and worked. Miriam Hetzel's pottery in a small building was both home and studio where she sold her work. Sculptor Marcus Aurelius Renzetti (known as "Renzetti") occupied a former ice house at the edge of the creek bordering Arden on the north. Writers, artists, craftsmen, actors—all were attracted to Arden by its dedication to the arts and crafts.

Most residents commuted to work in Philadelphia or Wilmington by bus, car, or train. The Baltimore & Ohio Railroad ran north and south at the eastern edge of Ardentown; the Pennsylvania Railroad, which traversed the length of the Eastern Seaboard, stopped in nearby Claymont. When I lived there the roads had been paved, but there were no sidewalks, no street lights. We walked in the narrow, two-lane road and moved to the curb when a car came along. We knew the roads like the palm of our hand and could walk across town and back on the darkest of nights. In fact, as kids we welcomed the dark so that we could duck out of sight of the few cars that came along. Footpaths between houses and main roads provided pedestrian-friendly shortcuts.

By the time we moved there, Arden's population numbered about 500 residents, limited beyond that by regulations that prohibited subdivision of land. Two adjacent tracts, Ardentown and Ardencroft, were added later. In Ardentown annex, the Robin Hood Theater flourished with plays brought by a professional theater company that attracted audiences from Wilmington and Philadelphia and provided a few summer jobs for Ardenites.

The Gild Hall was the gathering place for the town's many activities—Saturday night suppers, folk and square dances presided over by the inimitable Earl "Pappy" Brooks, or ballroom dancing with a live band or recorded music. There was a folk festival every year in the Hall. The Arden Fair on Labor Day weekend featured indoor and outdoor booths with handmade goods, kids' activities, and exhibits of everything from pottery-making to iron forging to weaving on a loom on the grounds around the Hall. The Fair's climax was a big dance that drew everyone in Arden and relatives and friends from as far as New York and Washington.

Arden had a more stable community life than any place I've ever known, and all my life, consciously or not, I longed for something like it again. Those eight years, from nearly 11 till 18 and out of high school, were imprinted on me forever. At the same time, I was aware of living a kind of double life because of the sharp contrast between that small village and the neighboring towns where I went to junior and senior high school. At home, there was the fertile soil that embodied the values, beliefs, and lifestyle of my parents and friends. Outside Arden was a different world.

Folk songs were my religion

I heard folk music not only at the festivals and special events at the Gild Hall, but also at campfires in the woods, where people of all ages sang together with guitars and a banjo and mandolin. We roasted marshmallows and sat or lay on blankets on the ground and watched the smoke curling up through the trees while we swapped songs. Some drank beer out of bottles kept cool in the creek. There were the recordings I heard at home and at friends' homes, music recorded in the 30s and 40s by folklorists and small record companies—gospel, blues, Southern mountain ballads. My girlfriend Elaine Lanciano and I sang together in close country harmony many of the songs we heard on records and learned from others at those campfires.

Some of us went to nearby Sunset Park to hear Roy Acuff and the Smoky Mountain Boys, Charlie and Bill Monroe, and other Grand Ol' Opry favorites. At Christmas, a group of people went from door to door singing Christmas carols, including secular carols from pre-Christian traditions. We were greeted at neighbors' doors and often invited to warm ourselves with eggnog or mulled cider.

We also heard the anti-fascist songs being sung during World War II—songs of the Lincoln Brigade and others too controversial to be issued by the big record companies. Huddie Ledbetter (Lead Belly) came to do a concert at the Gild Hall not long after he had been pardoned by the Governor of Texas, "discovered" by John and Alan Lomax, released from prison, and had gone to New York City. Other performers who came to Arden were Josh White and Richard Dyer-Bennet, known to Arden folks by their recordings and appearances in Philadelphia and New York.

A highlight of my last summer in Arden, 1946, was meeting folk singers Pete Seeger and Lee Hays when they came to do a concert at the Gild Hall. Both had been members of the Almanac Singers who had traveled and sung for the labor movement during and after World War II. After meeting Pete and Lee and hearing about People's Songs and its mission "to publish and distribute songs of the people," I knew that this music would be central to my life from then on. That year I also went with Amy and friends to hear Paul Robeson in a concert at the Philadelphia Academy of Music.

Arden wasn't a place I wanted to get away from, and in the summer there was so much going on that when my parents said they were going to the seashore, or to visit relatives out of town, I begged to stay behind. Most of my best friends lived in Arden only during the summer, and we spent our days at the swimming pool in the creek, where I learned to swim and dive. We went to the Water Festival on the 4th of July, and everybody gathered at the pool on summer days. There were dances and plays and concerts at the Gild Hall; the Pig 'n' Whistle where we bought ice cream cones for 10 cents; campfires in the woods; and lots more. During the rest of the year I went to high school in Wilmington, but I lived for summers in Arden.

Adolescence and family relations

Amy was active in community affairs, and for a year she was president of the Arden Club. She wasn't a big organization person, but she got along with everybody and everyone liked her. Henry, meanwhile, was building a real estate business in suburban Philadelphia and at first he would drive 30 miles up and back every day, but when gas and tires were rationed during the war, he was gone all week and came home on weekends. After dinner on Friday night he often retreated into reading the newspaper, or maybe walked around our quarter acre of lawn and woods with his hand-carved cane. He could be very sociable at mealtime or family gatherings, or the parties my parents gave, but his growing physical limitations, along with the demands of work and financial responsibility, accounted for his solitary behavior when he was at home. He suffered from asthma and allergies and took medications for cardiovascular conditions, all of which were factors in his inability to take part in Arden activities. He left that up to Amy, who was deeply involved in community life. He certainly wasn't the father that I wished he could be, and I suffered from his increasing lack of interest and participation in my life. During the school year I recall being bored and restless on Sundays after my school work was done, with Henry behind his newspaper in the big arm chair, listening to opera or classical music when I longed to play folk music or jazz records or invite friends over.

I sensed that my father was changing, becoming more middle class, moving away from the early radicalism and liberalism of earlier years. He saw some of our friends in the community as "freeloaders," enjoying the big parties at our house with plenty of food and liquor, taking advantage of his hospitality. There was a lot of drinking at those parties. I remember sitting on the stairs after I was supposed to be asleep, and when I couldn't stand it anymore yelling, "Please be QUIET!" I felt left out by the same adults who treated me as an equal in their homes and in Arden activities.

Free love, or open marriage, was acceptable to some Arden residents, in theory if not in practice. At parties I glimpsed married women sitting on men's laps, a single man who was quite popular with other men's wives, and such. But some of those same people were also mentors for me as I was growing up and finding my way. Some gave me more support than my parents as a young person with a mind and a keen interest in the world. I saw them as interesting people who lived their lives and beliefs, whether the larger society approved or not, and found in Arden the freedom to be diverse individuals. All my parents' friends were actively involved in Arden community life.

Junior High and High School

After 6th grade in the two-room Arden schoolhouse, students had to be driven to school by parents until we were old enough to ride the bus between Wilmington and Arden. Amy was part of the car pool. I went to Claymont Junior High School in 1941, two miles away in a working class, industrial area near the Pennsylvania border. I remember the day that Pearl Harbor was attacked. The news came over the loudspeakers in class, and we were all sent home. After 7th grade, I went to Mount Pleasant Junior High in a middle class suburb of Wilmington. It was quite different from either Arden or Claymont, and I don't remember much about school. I do remember that I had "an accident" at a party at one of the kids' homes. We were playing Post Office, a kissing game, and I felt so nervous and out of place with these new, strange kids that I wet my pants standing behind a chair. It was terribly humiliating, and I ran upstairs and told the mother, who came to my rescue and drove me home.

That experience was akin to recurrent dreams where I have to go onstage without knowing my lines. I did feel scared and self-conscious a lot, but I pushed through it. I'm sure that junior high school is hard to recall because my life in Arden was so completely different. There was a Home Economics class in which I made apple sauce and did something with a sewing machine. I did not feel much in common with the other girls. Life at school was like dues I had to pay—not what I chose or liked or wanted to be part of.

Early class consciousness

There were low-income people in Arden, but class differences weren't so much about wealth and property as about behavior and lifestyle and interests. Though some took part in community life, the working class people in and near Arden were not part of the "in group," and there was an often unspoken, condescending attitude toward people whose language was colloquial or who worked in the nearby industries. Kate was an Arden woman who was friendly and warm, but it was clear that was considered "less than" my parents' friends, not only because she was poor, but because her house became a hang-out for many of the teenagers. It was rumored that she had affairs with teen-age boys.

The class divide that I saw in Arden made me understand that Arden people did not always walk the talk. The contradictions between the ideal and the reality were as true in Arden as anywhere else. Going to school and having friends outside of Arden made me aware that, despite the professed liberalism of my family and their friends, Arden was not immune from the hypocrisy of the larger society. The gap between people's social theories and their social practice could be as great in Arden as anywhere else.

I trusted people wherever I found them. I couldn't find it in myself to believe that people were evil or had evil characteristics. Later I learned in many ways a lot about the many factors that influence people to be who they are and do the things they do.

When I was 12 or 13, I remember bringing some boys from Claymont to the Arden Pool as guests. I thought they were terrific. I think I liked them more and wanted to find out more about them because they were different and considered inferior by Arden values. There was a snobbish attitude toward these kids who literally came from the other side of the tracks. (The railroad bordered Arden on one side.) I wanted to show Arden people that they were mistaken about these outsiders and I needed to demonstrate my beliefs by putting them into action. I began doing things, saying things to educate others, showing there was another way. I was "learning by doing" and influencing others in the process.

In high school I was drawn to boys who were on the sports teams, working class boys. Two of my favorites were Irish—"Peanuts" Riley and "Belchy" Walsh! I would invite my classmates to parties at our house, and they were amazed. They had all heard that Arden was this exotic place—a nudist or free love colony, a Bohemian stronghold. The kids had a ball at my parties, dancing and socializing among peers who didn't fraternize at school. And as a teenager, I had a normal need to be part of my peer group. Aside from my parties, though, the Wilmington kids rarely came to Arden.

Despite the mediocre public school education, I continued to get good grades. Except for math—when I got past arithmetic and algebra, I got mostly Ds instead of the As and Bs in other subjects. I hated Home Economics, the cooking and sewing classes. In that respect I was like Amy—the domestic work expected of girls and women was never my favorite.

Living in two worlds

High school was more interesting when I made the cheerleading squad, after practicing and trying out. It took a lot of nerve because I didn't consider myself pretty or attractive. I compared myself unfavorably to the other girls and felt self-conscious about physical attributes that were "different" from other girls—thick, curly black hair, a long nose, small breasts and wide hips. But cheerleading put me in the public eye. It made me feel like I could be part of something that was more up front and active than the classroom. In Arden I had sung with others and participated in community activities, and I needed to be visible at my high school in Wilmington.

As part of my college preparation course, I focused on English, three years of Latin, two of French. Math and science were a struggle, but I liked World Geography with a good teacher who showed how varying physical environments influenced people's social and economic life and history. It was the closest thing to Anthropology, my chosen major when I went to college years later. In my senior year, there was a Music Appreciation class in which the teacher let me play records to illustrate my talk on folk music and jazz. It was a precursor of a course I developed much later on Labor History in Songs, with songs and recorded music on the history of American folk and labor songs.

But in the high school years, 1943-46, during and after World War II, the most memorable things happened outside of school. On weekends I went to Philadelphia by train to hear jazz and folk music. During summers in Arden, I enjoyed activities with older friends who opened up worlds of literature and music and ideas. I lived for Arden summers. Bill Pressman, a summer resident and musician, taught me my first guitar chords and encouraged me to buy a Martin guitar. He was a central figure at the campfires at Indian Circle in the woods, and he even came to Arden during Christmas holidays to lead our carol singing!

In 1945, the summer I was 17, I was infatuated with Walt Miller, who was 26 and one of the older summer crowd. He had been in the Army, stationed in South Carolina. He gave me his copy of Thomas Wolfe's first novel, *Look Homeward, Angel.* I still have it, with Walt's handwriting inside the cover: "1945–Walter B. Miller–Columbia, S.Car." Once we went for a drive in his car and talked about all kinds of things. On the way back we had a necking session, parked on a narrow Arden road near home. When Amy found out, she went to talk with Walt, warning him about how young I was and not to make sexual advances. I was angry and felt betrayed that she had talked to him privately instead of me. So that settled that. Walt and I never went out together again.

That year, besides *Look Homeward Angel,* I read Upton Sinclair's *The Jungle* and John Steinbeck's *Grapes of Wrath,* two books that strongly influenced my life. Elaine Lanciano and I drifted apart when I started hanging out with the older crowd, and she became the "leader" among the Arden kids our age. During the school year she lived in Philadelphia, and when I moved to that city in 1946, we reunited and sang together again.

Segregation, racism, and World War II

Delaware, just below the Mason-Dixon Line, was segregated and there were no people of color living in Arden. Schools were segregated, city buses, hotels, movie houses. In my junior year at high school, I joined an interracial group run by an Arden Quaker, Fritz Geissler. We met at the YMCA in Wilmington, only two blocks away from the DuPont Hotel, the big business and visitor center of the city. We gave out leaflets to protest segregation in movie theaters and hotels and on buses. I became very vocal in wanting my high school to play team sports with Wilmington's black high school—not even integration, just let's play the black high school team—and that made me an outcast. One girl, Mary Grant, a Catholic, remained my friend, as did a couple of Jewish boys who shared my interest in modern jazz. When, in my third year as a cheerleader, I was supposed to become squad captain by seniority, the girls on the squad decided to hold a vote and I lost out. I was deeply hurt and came home in tears, but Amy comforted me and urged me to stay with it, and I remained on the squad till the end of my senior year.

During that period, I invited Sam Moon, an African American friend I'd met in the interracial group, to come to visit me in Arden. I was furious when I learned that Amy and a friend had gone to meet the bus to tell him not to get off. He wasn't on it, probably because his family had refused to let him make the trip. But I was outraged. It was the first case of real betrayal that I had felt from my own family. Their story was that they were looking out for me—not for themselves, of course!

That incident happened during World War II, a year or two after there had been a cross-burning in Arden on the lawn of the schoolhouse across from our home. We didn't know who had done it, but after a big town meeting called by Arden president Buzz Ware to bring it out in the open and discuss this racist act, we learned that it had been pulled off by the teenage son of one of Arden's upstanding families. I remember the debate about whether this incident was just a boy's prank or the result of his family's racist views. We had had black people come to various events either as guests or performers, but after all, this was segregated Delaware. And there were people in the Arden community who didn't see eye-to-eye with the liberal views of the elected leaders. As a result of the open forum that brought the cross-burning to the attention of the entire community, the boy's family sent him away to school. I don't recall ever seeing him again, though his parents continued to live in Arden.

To me, the cross-burning incident underscored the contradictions inherent in a small community of principles and ideals trying to exist within a hostile environment; how nothing and no one is immune to the influences of the surrounding society and culture. Arden was run by town meetings, either monthly or quarterly, held at the Gild Hall and open to all residents. People were vociferous in their views, and they certainly weren't all of one mind; in fact there were strong opinions on the whole range of community issues. I heard stories about people throwing chairs and being pretty rowdy at those meetings. Decisions reached were published in the monthly *Town Crier* by

Billy Hutchison, who ran the Arden Press. Billy shuffled around town in old, baggy clothes that smelled like the old pipe that was his trademark. He was the one citizen that our dog, Funny, would not tolerate because of his funky smell and his Charlie Chaplin shuffle! The year that Amy was president of the Arden Club, Billy was a frequent visitor at our house—and she had to tie up the dog when he came around. Once Funny ran to an apple that had fallen off our tree and devoured it rather than leave it for Billy Hutchison!

During World War II, divisions among Arden residents surfaced, as feelings and opinions ran high on everything from anti-fascism to rationing of gas and tires and food. The family car had a sticker that declared what level of priority you had at the gas pump. We saved string and all manner of materials and gave them to the "war effort." Amy and I were trained as airplane spotters to look for enemy aircraft. We signed up on rotating shifts with other residents to climb a little water tower in Ardentown and scan the skies with a telescope. That was quite an experience, my first participation in fighting fascism.

As time moved on and people moved in and out of Arden, it was no longer the close-knit village, the visionary community of the founders, but a mixture of old-timers who had lived the history and newer folks who brought with them diverse backgrounds and values. But unlike other small towns, the land trust with its keepers, the Arden Trustees, the fundamental town structure and governance, and the prohibition against commercial interests invading it, provided a stability over time that few communities are able to sustain in the face of changing times.

Meanwhile, at home

When I was 16 my parents had their first big fight. It was loud and scary, and I was right there to witness it. I don't remember what they said, but Henry stormed out saying he wasn't coming back, and Amy was in tears and broken up. I was terrified, seeing my mother as powerless for the first time. He did come back, full of remorse, before long. They must have faced the fact that they had both been having affairs, their lives were diverging, and for better or worse they weren't in love anymore. Their common-law marriage decreed that if they stopped loving each other, they would cease to live together. Twenty-two years later, that's what was happening.

The Potter Family, 1908.
Lloyd, 5; Cora; Ed; Amy, 4.

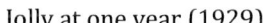

Amy Potter and Henry
Smolens in Arden in 1924.

Jolly at one year (1929).

Amy Potter Smolens with
Jackie, 2, and Jolly, 4.

Jackie and Jolly eating
watermelon on their wagon.

Jolly at 9 in her Easter outfit visiting grandparents Cora and Ed in Washington, D.C.

Amy during her year as President of the Arden Club, 1940s.

Henry at the head of the dinnertable, 1940s.

The cottage at Robin Hill in winter, 1934-39.

The house in Arden, home from 1939-46.

The Gild Hall in Arden, scene of Town Meetings, Saturday night suppeers, and diverse social and cultural activites.

CHAPTER TWO
You Don't Learn This in College

In September 1946, we left Arden for Philadelphia and moved into a house Henry had bought in Upper Darby, near his real estate business. My parents knew they were going different ways, but Amy was financially dependent, and both their future spouses were awaiting divorces as well. Besides, Jac was still in high school, and Amy wanted to stay at home until he had graduated.

Leaving Arden at the end of that summer was not without conflict. It had been my home for the crucial years of 11 to 18; I had found community and friends there. But I knew Arden wasn't big enough to hold me, that I had to move into the larger world of ideas and action. I had met Pete Seeger and Lee Hays in Arden and had heard other wonderful folksingers, and I looked forward to being in Philadelphia, helping to spread People's Songs and continuing on the path of singing and political activism. I was excited by the possibilities that lay ahead.

On the other hand, I had been sorely disappointed when I was not accepted by Temple University, and let down by my father's unwillingness to let me apply to other colleges, claiming that he could not afford to pay the cost of board and tuition.

I had taken a college preparatory course in high school—three years of Latin and English, two years of French, and other required courses. Toward the end of my senior year in the spring of 1946, still living in Arden, I had applied to Temple University, which was near enough to be able to live at home while I went to school. My interests in college were broad, but I had settled on Journalism as a major. I felt I had done well in the exams, except maybe on the math part, never my strong suit. During the summer I received a letter saying that I was not accepted, with no explanation. I felt as if the rug had been pulled out from under me. I went to the Philadelphia campus and made the rounds of deans' offices, knocked on doors, asked to know my scores and why I had been turned down. No one would give me an answer. I was left to assume that it was because of the quota system. Quotas weren't much talked about, but they were common for out-of-state applicants, females, Jews, African Americans. And since Roosevelt had signed the GI Bill of Rights in 1944, World War II veterans were given first priority. So there were numerous possible reasons, but no one would tell me anything—not even my test scores.

After the rejection by Temple, my older cousin Phyllis talked to my parents and encouraged me to apply to Black Mountain College in North Carolina, the small liberal arts college where she had gone. The man who interviewed me in Philadelphia explained that they accepted only 90 applicants a year. Soon I received a letter informing me that I was not accepted because I was not certain what I wanted to get from a college education—and this from a school that specialized more than most in the liberal arts. It was another slap in the face, closing the door on my last hope to go to college.

Joining the workforce

Trying to swallow my feelings of rejection by my father and two colleges, I dutifully went to work in Falkenstein's record store in Philadelphia. Amy had arranged with old Mr. Falkenstein for the job in the secondhand record department. I worked six days a week for $25/week, of which my father demanded $5 as my share of the cost of living at home. That's the way Henry looked at things—you help pay your way when you're old enough to go to work.

On the second floor where I worked, used 78rpm records were stacked on tables. My job was to separate the records by artist, keep them in piles on the tables, and help customers find what they were looking for—mostly classical and opera. George Falkenstein was a likeable character, and people would come in looking for records by Benjamino Gigli and Enrico Caruso and Tito Schipa. My interest was in the big bands of the 40s—Count Basie, Woody Herman, Benny Goodman, Artie Shaw, and their spin-offs in jazz trios and sextets. Falkenstein's carried a few such recordings, and some old-time folk music. I worked an 8-hour day, commuting by bus and subway to downtown Philadelphia.

I didn't drive then, and didn't learn to drive for another 33 years. Henry used the family car during the war, when gas and tires were strictly rationed, and when we moved to Philadelphia there was good public transportation. I traveled by bus, subway, and trolley, or got rides with people who had cars. A car was not a necessity, nor could I have afforded one.

The home scene at my father's house in Upper Darby was far from nurturing; in fact it was alienating. Henry was completely wrapped up in running his real estate business, seven days a week. Mary, his business associate and wife-to-be, was crazy about him and he often brought her to the house. Amy, cut off from the life she had known and loved in Arden, was biding her time until she could leave to marry Charles Cook. When she nearly died from complications of the mumps, I felt I might not live through it either. She was bedridden and weak and couldn't keep food down. The doctor came frequently (they still made house calls in those days) and the house felt like a hospital. I felt terrified and trapped in my room, going to work every day and dreading the nights.

Things were spinning apart for me; I was propelled outward whether I was ready or not. It no longer felt like home, and I didn't want to be there. I felt compassion for Amy, who didn't want to be there either except for the sake of us kids and her pending divorce. Jac called the house in Upper Darby a "decorated morgue" and spent most of his time in Arden, 30 miles away.

Carving out a life

Even then, at 18, I was aware of the dual nature of my life, very little of which was based at home. Evenings and weekends I was either going to jazz clubs with my Arden friend Elaine, or singing at meetings where I learned about progressive issues and politics. There was no overlap of these two areas. Elaine and I performed as a duo, in the style of traditional and contemporary folk songs we had learned from recordings, other musicians, and country singers performing in rural areas near Arden.

An older black man I met in the jazz scene was a promoter of events, and when I did some typing for him in a small office on South Broad Street, I learned a lot about what was going on around town. He made passes at me, but I did not return them, and I think he didn't want to get himself in trouble with a young white woman.

Elaine and I often were the only white women at bars that featured music in North Philadelphia or on South Broad Street. We'd sit at the bar and have a Tom Collins, and guys would hit on us, but we always left together. We traveled by bus and trolley, and usually went different ways at the end of the evening because I lived outside of West Philadelphia and she lived in "South Philly."

Going to hear music at these bars was always on my initiative. Elaine's parents disapproved of our activities, so she told them she was spending the night at my house. When they found out what she was doing, they forbade her to see me. I don't know how she talked them into letting us sing together.

Some of my adventures were risky, some downright dangerous. My first sexual encounter, at 18, was with a black actor backstage at a Broadway show that was playing in Philadelphia. It was strictly a thing of the moment, an attraction to the excitement of the theater. The next year I became pregnant after having sex with a white musician I had met at jam sessions. When I told my mother, she took me to a doctor who performed abortions. Typical of illegal abortions then, the doctor agreed to start the process with the clear understanding that the fetus would be aborted elsewhere or he would lose his license. We went from South Philadelphia to Upper Darby, where Amy still lived, while I awaited the outcome under her watchful eye. After that, she insisted that I get a diaphragm and showed me how to use it.

My parents were concerned about me, but they undoubtedly felt frustrated and helpless to change the situation. My father would get angry and call me a slut—the same father who had brought his paramour home while his wife and kids still lived there. But because I was working and supporting myself, there was little the parents could do to "ground" me. They never ordered me to stay home.

Walking the talk

Then there was this other part of my life—the activist singer with guitar who carried her beliefs beyond the confines of family, friends, and conversation. On the way to work on the subway I read pamphlets on Marxist theory and Herbert Aptheker's series of books on "The Negro Question," a pioneering analysis of racism based on US history that was left out of the textbooks. It gave me a way to understand what I had witnessed in Arden and Wilmington. I had been in an interracial group in Delaware, but now I was reading left-wing tracts and going to political meetings. After a few months I left Falkenstein's for Ryall's record store in Upper Darby, which was closer to home and paid $30/week for six days. I became better acquainted with modern jazz and bebop from the early Dial recordings of Charlie Parker and Dizzy Gillespie. One musician who came in to buy records was Gerry Mulligan, a baritone sax player I had heard at jam sessions. At the same time, I was meeting Communists and progressives at meetings and events I went to with the record store manager, and to get singing engagements through this network.

The big dichotomy was between going to hear jazz in nightclubs and meeting black and white musicians, and on the other hand, being among mostly white people who were committed to social justice. I was going to meetings, hearing speakers, meeting people who had a point of view that made sense to me, singing and leading songs. I sang at meeting halls, people's homes, and college campuses all around the city—and I read a lot. I was getting an education I would not have gotten in college. Singing and song-leading were my main interest, and I quickly learned new songs to add to my repertoire. I was part of what was happening, and it felt like a natural outgrowth of my Arden experience. I was walking the talk, acting on the radical ideas I had grown up with.

In 1947, at 19, I went to Washington with a delegation to see members of Congress about the Rosa Lee Ingram case. Ingram was a black sharecropper in Georgia who had been assaulted by a white farmer for trespassing when her livestock wandered onto his land. When she fought back his rifle fell to the ground and two of her sons came to her rescue and struck the farmer with his rifle. The blow killed him. After 13 months in jail, an all-white jury found them guilty of murdering the white man. The Ingram Case had won the support of the Communist Party and the Civil Rights Congress in their campaign to stop lynchings, murders, beatings, all racial injustice. I took my guitar and led singing on the train. Our delegation met with New York Congressman Adam Clayton Powell to lend support to his stand against racism and for civil rights.

That year I went to New York to be in the May Day Parade and marched with People's Songs—Pete Seeger wearing his Army uniform and playing his 5-string banjo, Woody Guthrie playing his guitar that proclaimed "THIS MACHINE KILLS FASCISTS." Huge contingents from labor and progressive organizations marched and sang all the way down Fifth Avenue to Union Square for the big May Day rally. I was in action with thousands of people. I was a part of all that was happening. I was doing what I was meant to be doing. The people on the Left, in the Communist Party, the labor contingents, the singers and speakers and marchers were my new community.

People's Songs

The big leap came in 1948, after I had worked in Philadelphia nearly two years. I had been inspired and energized by Pete Seeger and Woody Guthrie, the newly formed People's Songs and lots of young people, with headquarters in New York and branches being organized around the country. As a singer/activist, I had become part of the post-war progressive movement. Yearning to be at the center of things, I let Pete and the staff know that I wanted to come and work for People's Songs. They responded by offering me a job booking singers, musicians, dancers, actors and speakers for concerts and other events in the New York metropolitan area. They would pay $20 a week; the rest of my $35 salary was to come from bookings I would get for myself. And I would work five days a week instead of six, leaving weekends free to learn my way around New York!

Through an Arden acquaintance, I learned of a room for rent in Manhattan and in June, just before my 20th birthday, Henry and Jac drove me to New York and helped me move into my first home away from home. It was a walk-up on 52nd Street near Sixth Avenue, over a flamenco restaurant on what was known as "The Street" because of the many jazz nightclubs in that single block! What a coincidence—living in the midst of one form of music I loved, and working not a mile away for the organization whose mission was to "create, promote and distribute songs of labor and the people." Though I couldn't afford it often, I managed to go to the Three Deuces to hear Billie Holiday and Charlie Parker, and another club down the street to hear pianist Marian McPartland. (That entire block has long since been torn down and replaced by the Hilton Hotel.)

My room looked out directly onto 52nd Street, over the flashing neon sign for the flamenco restaurant downstairs. I shared the kitchen and bathroom with the woman in the next room—and the inevitable cockroaches that lived rent-free over every restaurant! The narrow room, with space for a single bed, bureau, and chair, was $10 a week—half my guaranteed salary, but less than a third if I got myself a booking for $15. (The only one I remember was for Mayor O'Dwyer at a house party on the North Shore of Long Island, where he requested that I sing "When Irish Eyes Are Smiling." Someone must have had the words, because I didn't know the verses, but everyone sang along enthusiastically.)

The People's Songs office was on the third floor of a West Side brownstone at 126 West 21st Street between 6th and 7th Avenues. From 52nd Street, I took the Sixth Avenue subway three stops to 23rd Street and walked from there. There was never a dull moment at work, with business meetings, editorial meetings, artists coming and going to sign contracts for their bookings, and the "hootenannies" where singers gathered to try out the new songs they had written for publication in the People's Songs Bulletin. "Hootenanny" became the popular term all across the country for an informal song-swap or singing gathering, a place for songwriters to introduce new topical songs. It was to folk music what "jam session" was to jazz. It wasn't so much about individual performers as about people making music together.

Fred Hellerman (later of the Weavers) came to visit me at 52nd Street, lugging his huge guitar case up the stairs to my room. I went with Pete in his jeep to find a fishing spear at a place he'd heard of on the Bowery. He and his wife Toshi hosted "hoots" in the basement of their Macdougal Street apartment, and at one memorable gathering, Lead Belly played my 6-string guitar, Freddie Hellerman played Lead Belly's 12-string guitar, and Pete played a washtub bass, while someone else played his 5-string banjo. When

I sang harmony to the songs Woody introduced at the 21st Street loft, he said I sounded more like him that he did! (No surprise, having grown up with his Dust Bowl Ballads.) Irwin Silber, People's Songs executive director, loaned me *What Is Philosophy?* by Howard Selsam, the first contemporary analysis of Marxist theory I had read. After reading it, I agreed that I was a materialist (dialectical variety), not an idealist!

I was one of few folksingers who listened to modern jazz and the new be-bop. There was a big disconnect between folk music and jazz in the minds of people on the left. Just as they tended to scorn the new abstract expressionist painting as "formalist" or "decadent" as opposed to the social realism that depicted workers and the class struggle, they judged modern jazz as abstract, individualistic, without a message, not understood by the average person. I, on the other hand, thought the folksingers were elitist, or blind, in their scorn of modern jazz and its African American creators, who were keeping it alive despite the lack of acceptance by commercial interests. One time I convinced Pete Seeger to go with me to the Royal Roost (later called Birdland) on Broadway near Times Square. He enjoyed it, and I introduced him to a couple of musicians I had heard in Philadelphia. Of all the folks in the People's Songs network, he had an open mind about music of all kinds, wherever it flourishes.

In July 1948 the Progressive Party Convention was held in Philadelphia to nominate Henry Wallace for President and put him on the ballot for the election that fall. So, from my new office job at People's Songs in New York, I booked Pete Seeger and other artists for the convention in the town I had just left! The convention was covered by CBS radio and television (still in its infancy), and journalists reported their amazement at the enthusiastic singing by the entire crowd gathered in Convention Hall. One soloist was Paul Robeson, whose rendition of "The House I Live In" by Earl Robinson, received a standing ovation from the audience of 30,000.

After the convention, Pete and Fred Hellerman and Tom Paley, a musician from New York, spent a night and day in Arden with friends of mine. Pete drove us back to New York in his jeep, and we sang all the way. It was risky there on the Jersey Turnpike when he steered with his knee so he could play his recorder with both hands!

The People's Songs Bulletin of September 1948 listed a 28-person staff, editorial board, and Board of Directors that included Bernie Asbel, Ben A. Botkin, Mario "Boots" Casetta, Bob Claiborne, Woody Guthrie, Herbert Haufrecht, Waldemar Hille, Ernie Lieberman, Alan Lomax, Paul Robeson, Earl Robinson, Betty Sanders, Pete Seeger; Irwin Silber; Win Stracke, Sonny Vale, and Jeannette Wells. Lee Hays wrote a regular column and Woody

Guthrie contributed songs and articles to the Bulletin, which was distributed nationally through local chapters and artists. Articles, songs, letters, drawings, and commentary came from singers, songwriters, and activists all around the country.

The folk process

The continuum of singing groups in the 20th century topical song movement went from the Almanac Singers (1940s, during and after WWII) to the Weavers (late 40s and early 50s), to Peter, Paul & Mary (1960s and 70s). The Almanacs predated the commercial age of recording and stardom. The Weavers made several folk-based recordings ("Irene, Goodnight," "Tzena, Tzena,") that rose to the top of the charts before the group was blacklisted. Peter, Paul & Mary came along at a time when folksingers were beginning to "make it" as commercially successful performing artists. With live, recorded, and televised performances, they were at the center of the 1960s Civil Rights and anti-Vietnam War movements with a repertoire that combined traditional folk songs with new songs that flowed from these struggles.

These three groups followed in the footsteps of earlier singers and musicians, black and white, rural and urban, who carried people's songs forward in the tradition of American "roots" music, in what Pete and others have called "the folk process." In every culture, this is how people pass along shared values, traditions, and experiences.

I hadn't been working there two months when People's Songs announced bankruptcy, and I was out of a job. I moved into an apartment on the Lower East Side with three other young women to save on rent. It was an eye-opening experience in the ins and outs of sharing living quarters with others. Two of us pulled our weight in paying the rent and upkeep, but the other two were unreliable and did not come through with their share of rent and responsibilities.

Tom Paley lived near the Manhattan Bridge, not far from our apartment, and I remember Tom playing his 5-string banjo as we walked and sang on the streets near the bridge. Once we were joined by Brownie McGhee, blues singer and guitarist who sang and recorded with blind harmonica player Sonny Terry. Tom later became one of the New Lost City Ramblers, keeping old-time country music alive with Mike Seeger and John Cohen. Brownie and Sonny have since gone to their reward.

Though Tom was not a songwriter, he was close to People's Songs because of its dedication to keeping traditional music alive while creating new songs in the never-ending "folk process." He understood the role of songs and

HENRY WALLACE and the Progressive Party Campaign of 1948

Henry A. Wallace had served for periods as Secretary of Agriculture, Vice President, and Secretary of Commerce during Franklin D. Roosevelt's administration. In 1948 he ran for President on a third party ticket against Democrat Harry S. Truman and Republican Thomas E. Dewey. His platform advocated friendly relations with the Soviet Union, an end to the nascent Cold War an end to segregation, full voting rights for blacks, and universal government health insurance. His campaign was unusual for his time in that it included African American candidates campaigning alongside white candidates in the American South and that during the campaign he refused to appear before segregated audiences or eat or stay in segregated establishments.

Source: Wikipedia, http://en.wikipedia.org/wiki/Henry_A._Wallace#The_1948 Presidential_election

singing in progressive politics. Old-time music, topical, political and labor songs, jazz, blues and other forms—to me it was all one thing: music. But the music that feels closest to my heart is still that old-time mountain music.

Barely two months after the move to New York, and two years after the move from Arden to Philadelphia, I was on my own in New York, sharing an apartment and looking for work. A friend got me a summer job as a relief counselor at a camp in upstate New York, charged with singing with the kids. I sat on a tree stump or in the dining hall as the kids gathered around and sang "Jenny Jenkins" and "The Fox Is on the Town-O" and "The Green Grass Grew All Around" and lots of other songs. It was great—but it lasted only a month. After that I worked briefly in a record store on 45th Street and then sold handkerchiefs at Stern's Department Store on 42nd Street.

In three short months—from booking artists at People's Songs, to camp counselor, to selling records and handkerchiefs!

The Wallace Caravan

In September 1948, I signed up to join the Progressive Party Caravans. Units of six or seven performers and a writer prepared to travel in 13 states, including some in the South, as part of the campaign to elect Henry Wallace as President and Glenn Taylor, former Senator from Idaho, Vice President.

As one of several units, we rehearsed our songs and created our skits in the basement of the party's headquarters at 39 Park Avenue. Herschel "Hesh" Bernardi, an actor with roots in the Yiddish Theater, headed the group I was in, which included his wife Betty and five other members, including a black woman, Juanita Griffin. Writer Ralph Lowe was an important member of our Caravan, collaborating with us on revising the script and our skits to fit local issues and historical data.

The Wallace Caravans were organized and led by professionals dedicated to "carrying the message of the Progressive Party to the people." Caravan units traveled by car, working with unions and other organizations to put on shows patterned after the "agit prop" (agitational propaganda) theater of the 1930s. Shows included songs, skits, and dances woven into a story narrated by one of the group, usually an actor. The objective was to illustrate in song and story the issues of the Progressive Party program—jobs and labor unity, racial equality, lower prices, decent housing, health care for all, and peace, at a time when the Cold War with the Soviet Union was heating up.

Somewhere amid the intense rehearsals, mealtimes, and meetings, Hesh convinced me to join the Communist Party. The people I rehearsed and performed with made up the cultural club I met with, and it felt like a family as I began to learn what it meant to be a Communist. Readings on Marxist theory and practice. Discussions on the role of culture in society. History of the class struggle and the trade union movement. Commitment to a program dedicated to creating a society run by the people who do the work. Between singing for a better world and embracing a cause I could believe in, I had found a home among comrades in words and action, meaning and dedication, and close friendship. This was my new community.

The Caravan leaders in New York set up contacts in the areas we traveled to, through local Progressive Party branches or through unions and other organizations. Among these were lodges of the International Workers' Order (IWO), an organization of nationality or ethnic groups representing immigrants who often spoke little English. We worked with progressive organizations among many ethnic groups.

After rehearsing for several weeks, our Caravan was assigned to go to Providence, Rhode Island. We drove nonstop, seven in one car, pulling a trailer with our luggage. No sooner had we arrived when a call came from New York headquarters saying they needed a guitarist in Pittsburgh. It seemed the guitarist who had been playing with the Pittsburgh Caravan was having health problems and was unable to perform. So I had my orders! I packed my bag, someone drove me to the airport, and I flew to Pittsburgh the very next day—my maiden voyage on an airplane.

In Pittsburgh I met a whole new group of performers, but as a Wallace Caravan that had rehearsed in New York, they were doing a lot of the same material. (The guitarist who had been depressed miraculously recovered upon my arrival, which gave this Caravan two musicians!) We traveled to towns built around steel mills and smelting furnaces on the Monongahela River and into West Virginia. We sang on sound trucks at street corner rallies, drawing a crowd to hear the message of Henry Wallace and the Progressive Party. Complementing a local speaker, our show was designed to draw a crowd and illustrate the campaign issues with songs.

At outdoor street rallies we sang songs written by the People's Songs network: "Vote for Wallace Election Day," "I've Got a Ballot," "The Same Merry-Go-Round," and "We Are Building a People's Party" (update of "Jacob's Ladder"). At union meetings and rallies we included "We Shall Not Be Moved," "Roll the Union On," and "Solidarity Forever," with words tailored to the situation. Issues for workers were jobs, speed-up, red-baiting attacks on unions and their leaders, decent housing, GI rights, racial discrimination by employers, and for a President who had taken a stand for coexistence and world peace. Wallace was running against Thomas A. Dewey and Harry Truman, and he was seen as increasing the chances of the Republican candidate, much as Ralph Nader was considered a "spoiler" for running on a third party platform in the 2000 election.

The Same Merry-Go-Round
By Ray Glazer and Bill Woolf

The donkey is tired and thin
The elephant thinks he'll move in
They fume and they fuss but they ain't foolin' us
Cause they're brothers right under the skin

CHORUS
It's the same, same merry-go-round
Which one will you ride this year?
The donkey and elephant bob up and down
On the same merry-go-round

The elephant comes from the north
The donkey may come from the south
If you look you'll find the donkey's behind
But they've got the same bit in their mouth

The donkey and elephant plan
To keep their control of this land
But don't let them fool you, divide you and rule you
Cause we have a much better plan

If you want to end up safe and sound
Get off of that merry-go-round
To be a real smarty, just join the new party
And get your two feet on the ground

A different kind of education

We met wonderful people and stayed in workers' homes, never in hotels. It was all worked out by the Progressive Party with local union organizers and IWO leaders. From Pittsburgh we traveled in Ohio, where we performed at meetings and on the streets in several industrial towns. In Mansfield we were arrested as we were singing on the sidewalk near the huge Westinghouse plant. The company had called the police, who accused us of blocking traffic and took us to the local jail. In our cells overnight, we sang, danced, made up verses to songs, and generally livened up the jail. Nobody slept that night.

The United Electrical Workers Union (UE) bailed us out the next day, pending trial, and we put on a rousing victory show that night for a crowd of unionists. The trial was postponed until after the election—when the issues that were too dangerous to sing about would no longer be a "threat" in that company town. We returned to Mansfield for a pre-trial hearing that was my first and only courtroom experience as a defendant. I clearly recall the anti-Semitism of the prosecutor, who insisted that I repeat and spell my Jewish last name clearly and asked me pointedly what kind of name it was. In defense of our so-called illegal sidewalk occupation, I said we were exercising our right to free speech under the First Amendment. After he put us on the stand separately in the hope that we might contradict each other, the judge dismissed the case for lack of evidence. It seemed that our performance on a little-used sidewalk beside a six-lane street had clearly not blocked traffic!

From Mansfield, we went to Akron, a rubber manufacturing center, and Canton, where we performed at meetings in IWO lodges. We arrived in Cleveland in time to participate in a large demonstration organized by the National Negro Labor Council demanding Fair Employment Practices by industries that discriminated against Negroes. Speakers included leaders of the United Packinghouse Workers; Electrical, Radio & Machine Workers; Mine, Mill & Smelter Workers; and Auto Workers—unions that were threatened with expulsion from the CIO because of their supposed Communist affiliations. The police Subversive Activities Unit was there in full force, scanning the demonstrators and protecting the bosses' interests.

I was getting a powerful, firsthand education as a young woman in the real world during the years I might have been studying in an academic setting. It was a seminal experience, working collectively with dedicated people who were practicing what they preached. My horizons were expanding, and I was finding community in many ways.

Back to the drawing board

After the election, in which Wallace won only one million votes, we returned to New York, "bloody but unbowed." There was no apartment to return to, and I had no idea what was coming next. But one Caravan—the group I had left behind in Providence, wanted to continue performing and working together after the campaign. Our objective was to go on the road again, this time hoping to find a progressive union that would hire us to help promote a program for workers' rights, anti-discrimination, and world peace. During the next seven months, I lived out of a suitcase, staying with Caravan members or acquaintances in Manhattan, Brooklyn, and the Bronx. Later I counted 13 different addresses where I had stayed in a period of 18 months in New York—not counting on the road. It felt like an extended family, almost like a commune, despite the frequent changes of sleeping quarters!

During that time, I was in love with Gene Bass, a man my age and a member of the post-election Caravan. We shared an apartment for a brief time in Lower Manhattan. Just before our Caravan was to leave on tour, Gene announced that he would not be going. His parents had put the pressure on to stay and work in his father's business, and though he was torn, he gave in and went home to his family. I was completely devastated and brokenhearted. Gene was the first man I had met who so completely shared my values and interests—a soul mate I genuinely loved and whom I might have married under different circumstances.

From November 1948 through June 1949, our Caravan group wrote, rehearsed, worked out material, and performed for different organizations in the New York area. The bookings we got were a good way of trying out the show we hoped to take on tour. In the spring of 1949, a union official who had seen a Caravan in action during the Wallace campaign wrote us from Iowa that his union wanted us to work with them on a tour of Iowa and Nebraska that summer. Clive Knowles, District 3 Director of the United Packinghouse Workers of America, was heading a farmer-labor cooperation program in the Midwest and worked closely with Fred Stover of the progressive Iowa Farmers Union. We were to work closely with the educational department of the UPWA in developing a traveling show around issues that connected the farmers who raised livestock with the workers who processed meat in the packing plants.

As with the Wallace Caravans, this was to be a subsidized tour. Our travel and living costs, including medical expenses, would be covered by the union, which planned the tour and accompanied us to the locations where we would appear with the union. There was no question in our minds about this arrangement. We were committed to the mission of "bringing culture to the people." For us it was a cause worth working for and we valued the experience. (Even so, Woody Guthrie wrote me expressing his objection to our working without pay, especially for a union.)

In a sense, it was history in the making, the last time this kind of tour could have happened in the Cold War period. As the "red scare" McCarthy witch-hunts escalated, the curtain rang down on any such cultural enterprises. Unions received the full impact of red-baiting and labor leaders either conformed or were thrown out of the CIO. Artists in film, theater, and the media were blacklisted when they spoke out against the anti-Communist crusade launched by Washington and Hollywood.

On the road again

We drove all the way to Iowa, with a stopover in Chicago to meet with some union leaders and do a show for hundreds of Packinghouse Workers. The Chicago stockyards were the biggest industry in that crossroads of East and West, United States and Canada. Chicago was the hub for railroads and shipping via the Great Lakes. We started meeting with UPWA educational directors who had close relationships with farmers' unions. Learning about the issues important to workers and farmers in the post-war years enabled us to develop the script we would use in the Midwest tour. That work continued in Iowa, as we met and talked with union leaders in each town on the tour, and learned about the history of the local union and the farmers,

The Iowa Farmers Union in the Depression, WWII, and Beyond

The biography and papers of Fred Stover, Iowa native and farmer, provides authentic background to what we learned on our 1949 Midwest tour. His experience speaks volumes about farmer-run organizations (cooperatives and unions) and how some were targeted during the effort to silence opposition to the Cold War.

When he was director of the Corn-Hog Program in Iowa in the 1930s, Stover said: "We put everything we had into organizing that corn-hog program and those early meetings. When the elected township and county chairmen called a meeting, nearly all farmers came. It was like getting a rebirth of democracy in every township in the land. It was a wonderful thing. And the farmships supported the program."

During his tenure with federal government agencies during the 1930s, Stover became interested in the Iowa Farmers Union, a progressive farmers' organization and local branch of the National Farmers Union. One reason for his resignation from the U.S. Department of Agriculture was . . . to return to Iowa and help build up the union there. Although the IFU drew in members from across the political spectrum (including, as he put it, "all kinds of right-wing dangerous elements,") Stover saw a powerful progressive element in the organization that he wanted to support in order to promote "the liberal fight for agriculture." In 1944 he was elected Vice-President of the IFU, and in 1945 succeeded anti-New Dealer O.B. Weber as the union's President. Said Stover:

"They [the members of the IFU] must choose whether the progressive and comprehensive program of the National Farmers Union and its cooperative programs and dynamic leaders are to receive our effective support as a people's movement, or whether individuals and interests hostile to our program are to be permitted to wield a frightening and dictatorial influence . . . whether we are to appeal to the many thousands of liberal-thinking farmers in Iowa and . . . start a strong independent and progressive farm movement in Iowa, or whether we are to appeal to the reactionary type of farmer."

Stover's tenure at the IFU was stormy and controversial. He was an outspoken pro-FDR liberal who originally shared these beliefs and had a positive working relationship with National Farmers Union President James G. Patton. The two

> supported the United Nations and a movement towards peace, and opposed a militaristic foreign policy and the increasing international arms race. They bothfought to end the disparity of income between farm and industrial economies and to preserve commodity price parity. [Things] changed in 1948 with the presidential candidacy of former Secretary of Agriculture and U.S. Vice-President Henry A. Wallace. Stover actively supported Wallace and aligned himself politically with the Progressive Party's campaign and platform. . . . This conflicted with Patton's perception of the Farmers Union as a nonpartisan organization that did not endorse specific candidates. Patton's insistence on a nonpartisan stance angered Stover, who believed Patton and the NFU were, in fact, behaving in a partisan manner against Wallace and against a firm progressive stand. He vowed that he would "not become either a conservative or a lukewarm sterile and frightened liberal just to accommodate a few people who have yet to demonstrate that they can and will build the Farmers Union." As Stover led the IFU towards an intensely progressive vision, he came into continued conflict with the . . . more mainstream NFU. He refused to give in to Red-baiting and attacks on his leadership of the IFU during the 1950s and continued to speak out for peace and against atomic war.
>
> Source: University of Iowa Libraries Special Collections, http://www.lib.uiowa.edu/spec-coll/

and the names of people and events that had taken place in each area. Those details brought the issues home to audiences of farmers and workers and moved them to join in our songs, laugh at the theatrical skits, and feel that the union and its Caravan understood their lives and conditions. Meanwhile, we were getting to know people everywhere we went.

In Waterloo, Iowa, we performed our program for a huge crowd of workers in front of a packing plant, on the site where a man who tried to cross the picket line had been killed during a strike years before. A photograph shows me facing this crowd with my guitar on a big flatbed truck. We could tell by the response that our message on the issues hit home to these meatpacking workers. We used the names of local people in our skits and songs. For me the experience had more depth and meaning than the Progressive Party tour. It was based on the history and conditions of a specific group of workers. The whole tour was grounded in the historical situation of the farmers and factory workers in that area.

We performed at 13 fairs in July and August—ten in Iowa and three in Nebraska, as well as union meetings in some of those towns. Our shows were held in big tents at these fairs, often right next to a race track (horses or autos), which was quite a challenge—when the racing cars drowned out our words we often had to pause in the middle of a song or a line. As we gave out flyers advertising our shows in front of the tent, we had a chance to meet and talk with farm families and invite them to see the show. One family with several children followed us from one fair to the next. They remembered the recent Great Depression, along with some of our songs, especially "The Farmer Is the Man" and "Passing Through."

Passing Through
Words: Dick Blakeslee Music: Traditional (Gospel)
© Sing Out Corporation

I saw Adam leave the garden with an apple in his hand,
He said 'Now you're out, what are you gonna do?'
Plant my crops and pray for rain, maybe raise a little Cain,
We're all orphans now and only passing through.

I was at Franklin Roosevelt's side just awhile before he died,
He said, 'One world must come out of World War Two,
Yankee, Russian, white or tan, young and old in every land,
We're all people and we're only passing through.

You don't learn this in college

The union took us through three big packing plants—one in Omaha, Nebraska and two in Iowa. In one plant sheep, hogs, and cattle were slaughtered and processed on assembly lines built in concentric circles—cattle on the outer circle, sheep next, and hogs on the inside circle. Workers were expected to slaughter 60 cattle an hour (one each minute). We heard stories about men flipping out and drinking hogs' blood due to the noise and the speed-up. It was a graphic education in what happens before the pork chops or roast beef get to the table.

In Arden I had read about the horrible conditions of the killing floor in Upton Sinclair's *The Jungle,* and here I was, seeing relatively better conditions because his exposé had spurred government regulation of the industry and, with years of union organizing, improved the lot of packinghouse workers. That book and Steinbeck's *Grapes of Wrath* were part of my basic education about industrial workers and farmers, and I was right in the middle of it—the farm belt and the industrial heartland of America.

A major emphasis of this tour was to reach the farmers who came to the county fairs during July and August with the message of Farmer-Labor Cooperation. The shows illustrated how the Meat Trust—four major meat packing companies—spent millions of dollars on keeping farmers and workers apart. By blaming farmers for high prices of livestock and workers for high wages on the job, the Meat Trust kept each group believing it was the other's fault in order to maximize their profits. Our message said that if farmers and workers saw their common interest, both would benefit.

During this period of intense activity and moving around, I wrote to Amy about my adventures and what I was learning. She had left Upper Darby and was living in Massachusetts with her new husband. I kept those letters, along with a few mementos I managed to save. We didn't see much of each other, but we corresponded through thick and thin. I recall writing to ask my father to send some prescription allergy pills (the same kind he used), as my hay fever was worse than ever on those grassy plains.

As the Caravan traveled in the Midwest, we met with local union organizers in each place. I became acquainted with one organizer who was both driver and guide, and we kept in touch by mail for several years after the tour. Our group met regularly to evaluate our performances, make changes in the script, and plan for the next location. The meetings were Caravan business combined with "educationals"—keeping up with Marxist theory and practice on tour!

After touring Iowa and Eastern Nebraska, we brought down the house in Chicago with a show for 3000 workers from the "Big Four" packing plants—Armour, Cudahy, Swift, and Wilson. After that, the union arranged for us to make a record based on the show we had done on tour. Weary and eager to return to New York, we recorded our show in a Chicago studio, directed by Win Stracke, a producer who had been a People's Songs board member. The two-record album, called "It's My Union," was distributed widely throughout the UPWA at cost for use "at local union meetings, community affairs, social gatherings and in your own home." The UPWA newspaper, The Packinghouse Worker, published a full-page ad promoting the album to its members. A veteran union leader called it "a historic document," the most effective union program he had heard in 40 years in the labor movement.

At this time, the House Committee on Un-American Activities (HUAC) was pulling all the stops to intimidate labor leaders and pressure unions to rid their ranks of alleged Communists. The UPWA was among several major unions, including the United Auto Workers, who were expelled from the CIO. Some years later, the UPWA was taken over by the Amalgamated Meat Cutters Union, which had survived the CIO's shameful purge of unions that were committed to democratic policies and would not cave in to McCarthyism. Many years later Les Orear of the Illinois Labor History Society (former head of the Amalgamated Meat Cutters Union) sent me a tape of the two-record 78-rpm Caravan album—from which references to UPWA and the entire song, "Passing Through," had been deleted during the McCarthy period.

Back in New York

Meanwhile, while we had been on tour, all hell had broken loose in New York. Paul Robeson had been prevented from singing at a concert in Peekskill by a mob of angry rioters as the police stood by and watched. The Left had mobilized and organized another concert in resistance to the ugly face of American-style fascists and rock-throwing racists uttering ugly epithets. Our Caravan performed at street rallies and marches in Harlem in the campaign to reelect Benjamin J. Davis, Communist City Councilman who had been jailed under the Smith Act. The newly formed Weavers also performed in that campaign, with Hope Foye, a black woman who predated Ronnie Gilbert. At a huge rally of thousands filling the streets at 125th & Lenox Avenue in Harlem, our Caravan climbed up on a sound truck after hearing a young actor named Bill Robinson recite poems by Langston Hughes and Margaret Walker. As we finished our songs, Paul Robeson and Ben Davis climbed the ladder, literally rocking the small truck with their combined stature!

. . . and on the road again

After a brief visit to my father in November, I rejoined the Caravan for a tour of small towns with the United Fur & Leather Workers Union in Central Pennsylvania and New York State, where they had organized the leather tanneries. While the union leadership was progressive, the membership in that area was more conservative, and there was no issue of farmer-labor cooperation, so we revised our show to fit the situation. Our tour coincided with hunting season, which was as traditional for these workers as the Catholic church, and our audiences, often at Elks Lodges and Odd Fellows Halls, were predominantly women, children, and older men. When we were invited to dinner at people's homes, we ate venison and rabbit, another new experience. Like the Midwest farmers and packinghouse workers, the people were warm and hospitable, and showed us their appreciation for bringing the union's message to their towns. I would never have visited these remote towns or met the people who make shoes, clothing, saddles, and all leather products—were it not for the strong desire of the Caravan, working with trade unions, to reach out to working people in their communities.

Jolly with an informal group at a People's Songs Hootenanny, New York, 1948. In the 1940s and 50s the Almanac Singers and The Weavers popularized folk, labor, and topical songs to audiences across the country.

The UPWA promoted the Union Caravan tour in the Midwest, Summer 1949. The program emphasized farmer-labor unity as well as peace and international cooperation.

The Fur & Leather Workers Union tour in Central Pennsylvania, Winter 1949, focused on labor issues and democracy. As in the Midwest, we traveled with workers and enjoyed their families' hospitality.

The Midwest Caravan shows were planned with the help of local packinghouse workers' and farmers' union leaders with their knowledge of the area's history. The shows also spoke to the need for peace and international cooperation as the Cold War heated up and union leadership was being threatened by the government's hunt for subversives in the "Red Scare."

At the end of the Caravan tour, we put on a rousing show for 3000 members of the UPWA in a huge hall in Chicago. After recording an album of the songs and skits (cover shown here), we returned to New York from an unforgettable summer.

CHAPTER THREE
Moves, Marriage, and Motherhood

The winter of 1949-50 was tumultuous—full of endings and beginnings and uncertainty about what lay ahead. After the Fur & Leather Workers tour I returned to New York, where our Caravan finally disbanded and we went our different ways. For a short time I stayed with Henry and his new wife Mary in Upper Darby while I pursued an invitation to go to Chicago and organize a union chorus. The plan was that I would stay in an apartment that was temporarily available, get a job in a packing plant, find a place to live, and organize a chorus for the meatpackers union. With no other work in sight, I thought why not use my experience to do something I really cared about.

This time the adventure turned out to be a disaster. In Chicago in midwinter, with sub-zero winds blowing off Lake Michigan, it took me five weeks to find a job. Plant managers, suspecting I was a union spy, asked why I wanted to work there or said I was overqualified. I was finally hired at a Swift subsidiary plant, fastening plastic whistles to the lids of peanut butter jars in a special promotion. About the only thing I remember is the relentless pace of the assembly line and the forelady whose job it was to see that we met our hourly quota. The temporary job was over in three weeks, and I was laid off.

There had been no time between job-hunting and trying to find an apartment in a strange city to even begin to organize a chorus, and my contact with the union was minimal. After eight weeks in Chicago and only three weeks' pay, I was broke and unable to pay rent even if I found an apartment. The last straw was discovering that I was pregnant after an encounter with the union organizer who had loaned me his apartment. In the icy chill of January, on this man's referral, I went to a doctor in a black neighborhood, but when the doctor saw that I was white, he said he was sorry, he couldn't help me. In utter despair, I called my father and told him I had to come home. He and Mary met me at the train and assured me they would pay for the abortion. Amy came from Massachusetts and accompanied

49

me to the same doctor I'd seen two years earlier. As before, he started the abortion process and Amy and I went to Henry's house to await its completion. Fortunately, there were no complications. But it was an abrupt and emotionally painful end to the Chicago episode, for all concerned.

Where do I go from here?

After having been on my own for two years, I asked Henry for help. His reply was, "You'll learn to make a living." He offered to pay for a secretarial course while I lived in his house until I found a job. I excelled in typing and shorthand and kept up my social and political activities.

Halfway through the 10-month course, Henry told me I would have to move out. The FBI may have approached him; at any rate he was not willing to face the consequences of having a Communist in his house. I knew he disapproved of my affiliations and the life I had chosen, so while this ultimatum came as a shock, it fit the pattern. I had felt betrayed by him since before we left Arden. He had had little time for his family, I no longer felt we were family, and it seems the feeling was mutual. I certainly didn't enjoy living there, with his new wife, knowing how he felt toward me. Nor did I want to be dependent. I found a job in a law office with the typing and shorthand skills I would put to good use in the years to come. I never took the second half of the secretarial course.

I found an apartment to share with a woman I had met in the progressive movement. Emi Tonooka (then Amy Morris) was a Japanese American who had been in the internment camp at Manzanar, and she was at least as opposed as I was to war and racial discrimination. The apartment was at 22nd and Spruce Streets in a residential neighborhood, at a rent we could manage together. My job with the Philadelphia lawyer was five days a week, and on evenings and weekends I took part in activities like singing at anti-war political events and getting signatures on street corners for the Stockholm Peace Petition.

Woody Guthrie wrote me long letters during the winter of 1950-51. They were full of erotic language and his urgent desire that I join a singing group he wanted to get together, "...a group that can stand up and lay down together better than those Weaver-y folks," as he put it. He was trying to recruit his old buddy Cisco Houston, and said he wanted to find a black woman to round out the foursome. One day in early January, I found an inscribed copy of his autobiography, *Bound for Glory,* at my doorstep, delivered by Woody on his restless rounds. Later I discovered the passionate love letter he had typed on the inside of the book jacket, written during increasing tensions with his wife

Cold War Censorship of Anti-nuclear Songs and Singers

After the Atomic bombings of Hiroshima and nagasaki on August 6 and 9, 1945, many people the world over feared nuclear warfare, and many protest songs were written against this new danger. The most immediately successful of these post-war anti-nuclear protest songs was Vern Partlow's "Old Man Atom" (1945) (also known by the alternate titles "Atomic Talking Blues" and "Talking Atom"). The song treats its subject in comic-serious fashion ("We hold these truths to be self-evident/All men may be cremated equal" or "I don't mean the Adam that Mother Eve mated/I mean that thing that science liberated") on serious statements on choices to be made in the nuclear age ("The people of the world must choose a thesis/Peace in the world, or the world in pieces!").

Folk singer Sam Hinton recorded "Old Man Atom" in 1950 for ABC Eagle, a small California independent label. Influential New York disc jockey Martin Block played Hinton's record on his 'Make Believe Ballroom.' Overwhelming listener response prompted Columbia Records to acquire the rights for national distribution . . . and it promised to be one of the year's biggest novelty records. RCA Victor rush-released a version by the Sons of the Pioneers . . .Bing Crosby was reportedly ready to record "Old Man Atom" for Decca when right-wing organizations began attacking Columbia and RCA Victor for releasing a song that reflected a Communist ideology. According to a *New York Times* report on September 1, 1950, "Those who protested the song's issuance on records insisted that it parroted the Communist line on peace and reflected the propaganda for the Stockholm 'peace petition,' Mr. Partlow said yesterday . . . his song was 'not part of the Stockholm or any other so-called peace offensive . . . It was written five years ago, long before any of these peace offensives.'" Buckling under pressure, both Columbia and RCA Victor withdrew "Old Man Atom" from distribution.

Source: http://en.wikipedia.org/wiki/Atomic bombings of Hiroshima and Nagasaki.

Marjory and his renewed urge to find a singing and traveling companion. But I had no wish to run off with a married man 16 years older when I was trying to settle down, and I gave him no encouragement. It was one of my wiser decisions.

By the spring of 1951, I had left the lawyer's office to work for the United Electrical, Radio & Machine Workers Union (UE), one of the progressive unions being hounded in the Cold War Red Scare. Unhappy about Emi's entertaining her boyfriend overnight in our close quarters, I rented a room in North Philadelphia with a family I'd met through my political activities. The neighborhood, known as Strawberry Mansion, is where Henry had lived when he visited Arden and met Amy. By now the community was interracial, with black people moving in as whites moved to more "desirable" parts of town.

My interest in jazz continued, and I went to hear music at clubs. Through people in the interracial neighborhood chorus I organized in North Philadelphia, I also met musicians in the new Rhythm & Blues scene. And I kept on singing at political events.

When I learned that Bill Robinson, the actor I had met in Harlem in 1949, was coming to Philadelphia in a theater production of "Rain," I went to see it. We renewed our acquaintance and stayed in touch after he returned to New York. Besides being a talented actor, he was attractive, outgoing, and fun to be with, and I fell in love with him. Seeking some stability in my life, I pushed for getting married. I would move into his New York apartment and do whatever it took to make the marriage work. The United Electrical Workers Union offered me a temporary job in its Manhattan office.

Friends who had met Bill tried to warn me of his drinking and drug use, but I discounted it. After all, my family and the Arden crowd had been drinkers, I had hung out in Philadelphia bars, and drinking was common among the people I knew. This was a man who returned my love, and whose life and interests drew me like a magnet. I wanted to get married and live in New York again, and no one could have stopped me!

It was about that time that my stepfather, Cookie, said about me, "Jolly sees trouble coming and walks right towards it!"

A port in a storm—or a stormy port?

In late June of 1951, I moved into Bill's apartment, up four flights of stairs in a tenement building at Elizabeth & Spring Streets, below Houston. Then, that neighborhood was called Little Italy; now it's part of SoHo. Everyone knew their neighbors, no one locked their doors, and the morning after our wedding we found a generous dish of homemade lasagna on the kitchen table! Saturday mornings, often before we were up, the ice man delivered a big block of ice to the blue-painted wooden icebox in the kitchen and collected the cash we left on the table. The icebox was next to the bathtub which, when covered by a board, served as a counter next to the sink. There was a tiny bedroom (filled by the double bed) with a window on the air shaft, and a living room with gas heater and two front windows that opened onto the fire escape. The toilet was halfway down the hall, shared by the 5th floor tenants.

Bill and I were married at City Hall on July 7, three days after my 23rd birthday. Bill was 26. Two actors we knew came along as witnesses. Bill worked nights as a dishwasher at the Village Vanguard while taking acting classes by day. The night after we were married, the Vanguard gave us a gala wedding reception, with dancing to music by the Clarence Williams Trio and songs by Eartha Kitt. (As she passed us on the dance floor, she whispered loudly to Bill, "Why didn't you tell me you were married?") I was happy and at home among jazz musicians and actors, black and white. We were off to a good start.

Orphaned as an infant, Bill had been raised in foster homes and never graduated high school. As a youngster selling newspapers on the streets of Harlem, he had frequently snuck into the Apollo Theater to hear the singers, comedians, and emcees. He easily picked up their styles and dialects and rehearsed the routines in front of the mirror in his room. At 17, he had enlisted in the Merchant Marine, had sailed the Atlantic and seen active duty in beachhead landings in Italy. He had a snapshot of himself with a small dog on board a merchant vessel.

Bill took advantage of the hard-won GI Bill to study at the renowned Actor's Studio. Morris Carnovsky, Howard da Silva, John Randolph, and other theater people encouraged him at a time when parts for black actors were all but nonexistent. The scope of his talent extended from Shakespeare to Langston Hughes, contemporary comedy to classic drama; the depth of his performance reflected his passion for life and learning. To hear him recite a poem or read a passage was a powerful, moving experience. I was devoted to this self-made man and his exceptional talent and wanted to do all I could to support his career. Aside from secretarial work, marriage was the most traditional women's role I had played in my own life drama to date—if marrying a black actor can be called traditional!

The beat goes on

When the temporary job for UE ended, I went to the Local 65 hiring hall to look for work. Local 65 (later District 65) represented dry goods workers in the Retail, Wholesale & Department Store Union (RWDSU). It was the first trade union to organize office workers. The hall was at 13 Astor Place, where I had sung in People's Songs hootenannies in the late 40s.

The first job they sent me to was in the office of Synthetic Plastics, a button manufacturing company at 42nd & Eighth Avenue. I lunched every day at the Horn & Hardart ("H&H") restaurant next door, where for about a dollar I could get a sandwich, coffee, and dessert. My next job, for a few dollars better pay, was at Klaber Bros., a garment manufacturer whose women's clothing, made by textile workers in the South, was distributed to retailers by workers pushing carts around the garment center in mid-Manhattan. Through people I met in a trade union club of the Communist Party, I learned something about strategy and tactics in the fight for democracy within a labor union. I took a class on Marxism with Howard Selsam at the New School for Social Research, and another with historian Herbert Aptheker on Negro History.

Within a year after we married, Bill and I moved from Elizabeth Street to an apartment on West 155th Street that was being vacated by activists who were leaving town to become "unavailable" to the witch-hunters of the McCarthy era. We moved in and I paid the rent under the existing lease. When the lease came up for renewal and we appeared as a couple, the landlord refused to sign it, and we had to fight for the right to live as an interracial couple in New York City on the border between Harlem and Washington Heights. We organized the tenants with the support of comrades and won the right to live in the apartment vacated by white friends.

The Committee for the Negro in the Arts (CNA) was doing a great job of putting on productions in Harlem at the Club Baron and other venues with black actors, singers, playwrights, and directors who could not find work in the "legitimate" theater. Among them were Ruby Dee, Ossie Davis, Lorraine Hansberry, Alice Childress, Harry Belafonte, Beulah Richardson (Bea Richards), Sidney Poitier, Claudia McNeil, Lloyd Richards, and Douglas Turner Ward. There were white actors, too, including John Randolph, Sara Cunningham, Lou Gus, Howard da Silva and others, some of whom had been blacklisted in the anti-Communist witch-hunts.

We took part in events organized by labor and progressive organizations in opposition to the House Un-American Activities Committee and its blacklisting of film and theater people on both coasts. At Harlem's huge Rockland Palace, I watched with thousands as Bill Robinson introduced the featured speaker and singer, Paul Robeson. Towering above Bill, Robeson put his arm around Bill's shoulder and said, "I want you to meet one of our fine young Negro actors."

That summer, Bill was hired as an actor on staff by Camp Unity, a left-wing adult camp near Wingdale, NY. So that we could be together, the camp hired me as lawn program director. After the victory at 155th Street, we looked

Senate and House Anti-Communist Investigations During the Cold War

The widely known term "McCarthyism" refers to the politically motivated practice of making accusations of disloyalty, subversion, or treason without proper regard for evidence. The term specifically describes activities associated with the period in the United States known as the Second Red Scare (also Red Scare), lasting roughly from the late 1940s to the late 1950s and characterized by heightened fears of communist influence on American institutions and espionage by Soviet agents. Originally coined to criticize the anti-communist pursuits of U. S. Senator Joseph McCarthy, "McCarthyism" soon took on a broader meaning, describing the excesses of similar efforts, such as reckless, unsubstantiated accusations or demagogic attacks on the character or patriotism of political adversaries.

During the post-World War II era, many thousands of Americans were accused of being Communists or communist sympathizers and became the subject of aggressive investigations and questioning before government or private industry panels, committees and agencies. Primary targets were government employees, those in the entertainment industry, educators, and union activists. Suspicions were often given credence despite inconclusive or questionable evidence, and the level of threat posed by a person's real or supposed leftist associations or beliefs was often greatly exaggerated. Many people suffered loss of employment, destruction of their careers, and even imprisonment. Most of these punishments came about through trial verdicts later overturned, laws that would be declared unconstitutional, dismissals for reasons later declared illegal or actionable, or extra-legal procedures that would come into general disrepute.

The most famous examples of McCarthyism include the speeches, investigations, and hearings of Senator McCarthy himself; the Hollywood blacklist, associated with hearings conducted by the House Committee on Un-American Activities; and the various anti-communist activities of the Federal Bureau f Investigation (FBI) under DIrector J. Edgar Hoover. McCarthyism was a widespread social and cultural phenomenon that affected all levels of society and was the source of a great deal of debate and conflict in the United States.

The House Committee on Un-American Activities (HUAC) became a standing committee in 1945. Under the mandate of Public Law 601, passed by the 79th

Congress, the committee of nine representatives investigated suspected threats of subversion or propaganda that attacked "the form of government guaranteed by our Constitutiojn."

Under this mandate, the committee focused its investigations on real and suspected communists in positions of actual or supposed influence in the United States society. A significant step for HUAC was its investigation of the charges of espionage brought against Alger Hiss in 1948. This investigation ultimately resulted in Hiss's trial and conviction for perjury, and convinced many of the usefulness of congressional committees for uncovering communist subversion.

In 1947, HUAC held nine days of hearings into alleged communist propaganda and influence in the Hollywood motion picture industry. After conviction on contempt of Congress charges for refusal to answer some questions posed by committee members, the "Hollywood Ten" were blacklisted by the industry. Eventually, more than 300 artists—including directors, radio commentators, actors, and particularly screenwriters—were boycotted by the studios. Some, like Charlie Chaplin, left the U.S. to find work. Others wrote under pseudonuyms or the names of colleagues. Few succeeded in rebuilding careers within the entertainment industry.

Studio executives told the committee that wartime films—such as *Mission to Moscow*, *The North Star*, and *Song of Russia*—could be considered pro-Soviet propaganda, but claimed that the films were valuable in the context of the Allied war effort, and that they were made (in the case of *Mission to Moscow*) at the request of White House officials. In response to the House investigations, most studios produced a number of anti-communist and anti-Soviet propaganda films such as *Guilty of Treason*, *The Red Menace*, *I Married a Communist*, and I Was a Communist for the FBI. The last was nominated for an Academy Award for the best documentary in 1951 and also serialized for radio. Universal-International Pictures was the only major studio that did not produce such a film.

Source: Wikipedia, http://en.wikipedia.org/wiki/House Un-American Activities Committee and http://en.wikipedia.org/wiki/McCarthyism.

forward to spending the summer in the country. I quickly took to the work of organizing activities that brought people together to hear lectures, dance, sing, and play games in the outdoor space.

In the course of my work, I saw firsthand, and heard from others, that racist policies and attitudes existed in the camp, sometimes obvious, more often subtle. Many blacks on staff were fed up, talking among themselves, and looking for ways to be heard. Some of the white staff saw the need to educate staff about racism and its effects, and for a better way of planning and carrying out activities. I met with staff and campers to discuss how policies could be improved, and toward the end of the summer I wrote up a proposal that we presented to camp management with recommendations for the following season.

Struggles within the Left

Having seen the struggle for democracy within unions, I was finding the same contradictions at a left-wing summer camp. It's the "immunity" that many nonprofits, churches and community groups plead to this day: "We're doing good work in the world, how can you treat us the same as other employers?" I was being educated in the dual struggle that exists—the one against the inequities of the capitalist system, and the one that's often found in organizations dedicated to improving conditions or even changing the system.

Meanwhile Bill, whose work involved rehearsals and performance for the evening entertainment program, was not involved in our meetings. He was the only black actor on staff and to some degree enjoyed his special status, but not without some underlying hostility. When he wasn't rehearsing or performing, he would often go to the nearby town and return late, leaving me alone in our tent, not knowing when he'd be back. I was upset by his drinking and how it changed his behavior. I was unhappy about the lack of closeness and time spent together.

Back in New York that fall, I got another union job in the office of Reliable Textile, a menswear manufacturer at 41st & Broadway. As always, I commuted to and from work by subway, a benefit of living and working in a city where the subway takes you from one end to another on the same (then 15¢) token. I became active in the progressive caucus working for democracy in the union—a major issue at a time when union leadership was conducting its own witch-hunt instead of defending the union from the Red Scare, in effect assisting rightwing forces in weakening the labor movement. When I ran for shop steward, I lost narrowly to a man who was backed by the union leadership.

In early 1953, I was walking home on 155th Street from the subway station when two men in suits approached me on the street. Before they had finished asking my name, I said flatly, "I have nothing to say to you," and kept walking. The FBI also called my employer, who told me of the call but did not fire me. That year huge rallies were held and international protest grew to halt the threatened execution of Julius and Ethel Rosenberg as traitors to the U.S. for allegedly having conspired to pass atomic secrets to the Soviet Union. I sang at meetings and rallies, and in June, I stood with tens of thousands of people in Union Square as we awaited word of last-ditch efforts to stop the execution. When the announcement came that the Rosenbergs had been put to death, an eerie moan arose, along with cries of shock and disbelief.

The plot thickens

Bill was driving a cab on a substitute basis and getting sporadic work in small theater productions, or as emcee at the big events being held to bring people together in the fight against the growing McCarthy blacklist and the Cold War. He worked at night and slept during the day, which meant that we didn't see much of each other. Our love life was nonexistent. Along with my job and union activities, I did what I could to promote his career, like negotiating fees for appearances as an actor or emcee when organizations expected him to work without pay to raise money for the cause.

Bill was hired to work at Camp Lakeland, another adult camp, for the summer of 1953. I stayed in the city this time, working at my job and visiting him some weekends. At the end of the summer I spent Labor Day weekend at the camp, and we talked about having a baby. As with getting married, it was mostly my idea, naïvely hoping to bring us closer by having a child. Sure enough, six weeks later I learned that I was pregnant, and at eight months, the workers at Reliable Textile gave me a gala baby shower as I said farewell to the job.

Thanks to union benefits on the job, I had good medical coverage during the pregnancy, including monthly check-ups with the doctor who would deliver my baby. I had no idea whether it would be a girl or a boy. My due date was June 3, 1954. Three months along, I nearly had a miscarriage and was ordered to lie flat on my back for nearly a week and to take Diethylstilbestrol (DES), a synthetic form of estrogen. (Years later, DES was proven to be potentially harmful to the fetus, if not to the mother.) On May 31, after eight hours' labor, a strong anesthetic, and two doctors to assist the breech birth, I heard one doctor say to the other, "There's a foot!" and Vicki Sue Robinson was born, a healthy baby weighing 6 lbs. 15 oz. As I awoke from the anesthetic, the nurse brought her to me, wrapped tightly, eyes closed. Bill, the proud father, exclaimed in awe, "She's a girl!"

A new chapter begins

When I got home with my newborn baby, Amy came to be with us for a few days, and Bill's sister Alice visited from the Bronx. They helped me as I learned to bathe Vicki Sue on the drain board by the kitchen sink. Her crib was in the bedroom, and I made a changing table on the bureau next to our bed. We had a small record player in the bedroom, and at a few months when she could pull herself up, Vicki would jump up and down to the music of Lead Belly's and Woody Guthrie's children's songs.

Bill drove a cab on the night shift to make his drug connections, and his addiction worsened. He tried to hide it, but when he locked himself into the bathroom, I knew he was shooting up. Once I heard him cursing as he threw his syringe out the window. If he was trying to quit, it didn't work, and things went from bad to worse. Much of that period is a blur, too painful to recall. It was clear that I could not depend on my husband to support us, and when Vicki was four and a half months old, I weaned her from breast-feeding, located a baby sitter, and took a full-time office job with Golding Bros. Textiles in Lower Manhattan.

Weekday mornings I got Vicki dressed and fed and prepared for the day, and wheeled her in a baby carriage some 10 blocks to the apartment of the baby sitter. After goodbyes and hugs, I walked to the subway and commuted a half hour to the job near Canal Street. The routine was repeated after work, except when Bill managed to pick her up from the sitter. I was away from my baby nine or 10 hours a day.

This time the job was non-union. I worked in a large office near the air-cooled room that housed the huge computer banks of the mid-50s, tended by technical specialists who got higher pay than the rest of us. I remember two men on that job—good-natured Marvin, my immediate boss, and Louis, a computer specialist, with whom I had a brief fling. As a woman of 26, a working mother with a marriage that was falling apart, I welcomed the attention of a man. I was doing everything I could do in my commitment to parenting and financial support. A life that was all work was too much to ask.

During her infancy, Bill and I sometimes took Vicki on weekends to the park at the end of our street, overlooking the Hudson River. We took photos of Vicki in the apartment and in the courtyard of the building. On her first birthday, wearing a bright red dress with a white bib, she looked the picture of health with her curly brown hair and happy smile. Occasionally we took her to visit Bill's sisters in the Bronx.

In early 1955, Jac and his wife Jean came to New York to visit and see

Vicki. Jean was in the late stages of pregnancy with their first child and, sure enough, she went into labor soon after they arrived. We rushed her to the nearest hospital, where she gave birth to Coby, the first of their four children.

Bill's addiction grew out of control, and when he forged some checks on friends of ours, it was the last straw. I had always kept in touch with Amy but had never told her about Bill's destructive habit. When I finally let both my parents know how bad things were, they came to the rescue. Vicki stayed with Amy and Cookie for awhile, and Henry paid for a lawyer I found through friends. In January 1956, I won an uncontested annulment in a Queens court. Not long afterwards Bill went to jail for forgery.

I quit my job and moved back to Philadelphia with 19-month-old Vicki Sue. Jac and Jean, who lived near Philly with their first child, took care of Vicki while I located an apartment, a child care arrangement, and a job, all within about three weeks.

Parkside Avenue

The one-bedroom apartment was on Parkside Avenue, a residential neighborhood in West Philadelphia near public transportation. My former roommate Emi Tooke, now married and with four children, lived a couple of blocks away. The child care arrangement I had made, in the absence of public child care in the 50s, was in the home of an older black couple who took care of several children during the week while the parents worked. I would take Vicki by trolley on Monday morning to Mrs. Kyle's, and pick her up on Friday after work. Getting on welfare was something I never considered. Sometimes I missed my daughter so much that I'd bring her home on Wednesday, keep her with me overnight, and take her back to Mrs. Kyle's on Thursday. It was hard for little Vicki to be torn between two homes.

My first job was in the office of the Hartmann-Leddon Chemical Company in West Philadelphia. I traveled by trolley or bus to work. The community-based Communist Party club I joined was devoted to organizing the Parkside Neighborhood Council. We met in people's homes and worked for a new public school, a youth program, clean blocks and safer streets, and a "friendly, cooperative neighborhood." We succeeded in getting a traffic light installed at a busy intersection. I sang at meetings in churches and schools and contributed to the neighborhood newsletter, news releases, and questionnaires. On weekends I'd take Vicki to visit friends, or to the large public park across the street from our apartment.

Sometimes on weekday nights, friends would come over for a pinochle game, or I'd get a baby sitter and go to hear jazz at one of the clubs I'd been to years before. A special treat was the Max Roach quintet with Clifford Brown and Richie Powell, before Richie and Clifford died in a tragic highway accident. I also heard Dinah Washington, Sarah Vaughan, Gerry Mulligan, the Modern Jazz Quartet, the Maynard Ferguson band, and other jazz musicians.

Once, when I went to try out for a chorus I'd heard of, I became acquainted with a woman who visited me soon after—wearing a man's suit. I was taken completely off guard and responded to her advances by making it clear in as friendly a way as I could that I was not interested in "that kind of relationship." It was the first time I had been propositioned by a woman. It was an unsettling experience.

Even more unsettling was being asked by a middle class black couple, whom I barely knew, whether I had considered giving up my daughter for adoption, saying they would be happy to give her a home. In a state of shock, I assured them that I would never consider giving up my child. I never saw them again, and it is still painful to think about. Once I tried to get help from a city government agency to locate a child care situation closer to home than Mrs. Kyle's house. The arrangement they found, right around the corner, lasted two days, after which the family reported that their child was too upset by having a strange child in the house! Vicki, on the other hand, had no problem adapting. She learned to get along in difficult situations and made friends wherever she went.

Billy Eckstine died today . . .

Billy Eckstine died today
    landmark of the '50s
    milestone on my rocky road
    "missed a Saturday dance...don't get around much anymore"
takes me back...
    Dinah Washington Ella Fitzgerald Sara Vaughan
    Max Roach Clifford Brown Richie Powell
the Blue Note in North Philly
    Showboat on South Broad Street
nineteen fifty seven
    years to come so far off
good times
despite hard-edge reality
    working for bosses
    trying to make it

        on my own
        with a child
        in Philadelphia
in the apartment on Parkside Avenue
the next-door neighbor
stands in the hallway
glaring, hands on hips
threatening my friends
black friends men friends
I take my daughter
by trolley on Monday morning
to Mrs. Kyle's house
and pick her up
on Friday evening
        torn in two
        mother and breadwinner
across the park to the trolley
feel her little body stiffen
when she gets too heavy to carry
        and I put her down
        and she screams and cries
        and refuses to walk
and I feel terrible and tired
        wit's end
        week's end
and try to put the parts of my life
together so she'll have
        one mother, not two
        one home, not two
and wish for the day when
there'll be one me, not two
or three
        mother
              breadwinner
        self
walking down 42nd Street
        shopping at the little grocery
        coming home from a meeting

look up at the sky through the trees
        and think how much beauty there is in the world
and how some day there'll be a better life
    for my little girl and me
hard to picture just how life will be different
    not looking too far ahead
      living and working and paying the bills
and on week nights
missing my little girl so much
her crib empty
thinking this isn't how I thought it would be
neighborhood meetings
pinochle games
somebody brings a bottle
laughter
occasional night out or
fling with a folk singer or jazz musician
friends struggling, too
on weekends, precious hours with
    curly-haired Vicki Sue
    wide-eyed, innocent child
riding her tricycle in the cement backyard
down a flight of wooden stairs from the kitchen door
    or "reading" her picture books aloud
    or scolding her "doll-baby"
    or going to visit friends who have children
her third birthday party
at a picnic table in the park across the street
friends and songs and games and ice cream...
and only three nights a week
my little girl sleeping in her crib next to my bed
my daytime persona
nine to five plus commute
secretary to a boss at a
    chemical plant
    dental manufacturer
    fund-raising office
    magazine
    direct mail shop

working for a paycheck
conscientious secretary
single mother
mustn't let them see the
    singer with guitar
    radical activist
    ex-wife of a black actor
    split
        fragmented
            role juggler
woman-in-search-of-herself.

My job at the chemical company ended when the boss fired me because I was "too friendly with the shop workers." I then found a job transcribing tapes in the office of a dental manufacturing firm, and heard union organizers chanting labor slogans outside the building through the head phones as I worked. From there I went to State of Israel Bonds, where I learned about writing news releases from a staff member. After a few months, my boss fired me for not lying to her superior when she took long weekends in New York, leaving me to cover for her. Finally, I landed an interesting job as secretary to the editor at *Greater Philadelphia Magazine,* where I worked closely with staff editors and learned something about magazine publishing. That job paved the way for future work as an editor. But with Vicki now in kindergarten, I wanted to spend more time with her, and I took a job closer to home in a direct mail house. It ended within months when I became ill from the extreme heat in the office and had to pay most of my salary for doctor bills.

In 1959, Lorraine Hansberry's play, "A Raisin in the Sun," opened in Philadelphia with Ruby Dee, Sidney Poitier, Lou Gosset, and other actors I had met in New York through Bill's theater activities. Standing with Lorraine Hansberry at the back of the theater, I congratulated her about the success of her play. It went on to Broadway and rave reviews, and was made into a movie that ranks with the winners in film history.

Powelton Village

Late that year Bill got out of jail. Wanting to believe that he would stay clean and sober and become a good husband and father, and I agreed that he could come and live with us in Philadelphia. (When I spoke with a man about helping Bill find a job on his release, he said, "You women are always trying to rescue some man." More words I wasn't ready to hear.) The reunion was initially a happy one for all concerned. I kept on working and Vicki had a father again. A photo shows him holding her in his arms in front of our apartment building.

In early 1960 we moved as a family from Parkside Avenue to Powelton Village, a community of single homes and apartments and tree-lined streets in West Philadelphia. I was attracted by the racial and economic diversity, and by the community spirit exemplified in Powelton Neighbors. It was a community with a history within a large, impersonal city. We moved into the second floor of an old three-story house that now had on apartment on each floor. My former roommate Emi Tonooka and her family had moved to a house nearby, and we soon met other families in the area. It was home and community for the next four years. Vicki turned five in 1960, went to a kindergarten in a public school, and stayed in the home of a neighbor's family until I came from work.

After the direct mail job, I was hired as secretary to the director of the Albert Einstein Medical Center, a long commute by subway across Philadelphia. This married man, scientist and head of a prestigious institution, lost no time in chasing me around his office and trying to talk me into accompanying him on trips abroad. In dismay after losing another job, I quit and paid an agency a week's salary for a job writing press releases in the publicity department of I-T-E Circuit Breaker Company, which had defense contracts. I'd worked there a year and a half when I was asked to sign a loyalty oath and a security clearance form. I discussed the situation with a progressive lawyer who counseled that I should decide based on my need to make a living. Nevertheless, I refused to sign the documents, and the company offered me a "non-sensitive" job for less pay. I turned it down and began another job search. John F. Kennedy was about to be elected President.

Editors I had worked with at *Greater Philadelphia Magazine* were starting up a new publication, *FM-Stereo Guide,* and they asked me to join them as editorial production manager. I loved being back in magazine publishing, but after six months the magazine folded and I was laid off. The Glass Bottle Blowers Association, an old-line craft union, hired me to work for its vice president, a job I was finally able to stay with until I chose to leave.

Learning the hard way

Bill was drinking again, and I would find bottles of codeine cough syrup here and there. He was borrowing money from our friends, and when he took the rent money I had earned, that was the last straw. On my lunch hour, on the verge of a breakdown, I went across town by trolley to see a therapist Bill had gone to just once at the urging of friends. He advised me that the odds were heavily against his changing and said, "Let's talk about you. What do you want to do with your life?" Through the fog of my exhaustion, I heard him. When I got home from work, I mustered all my strength and told Bill he had two weeks to move out—and despite fear of his angry retribution, I followed through by changing the lock on the door. It was one of the hardest things I'd ever done, and one of the best. Bill left Philadelphia a short time later. Vicki was seven years old and in public school. It was the second time she had been separated from her father. One of the most poignant memories of her at age seven is preserved in a snapshot I took of Vicki after Bill had left, standing by the gate in front our apartment, clutching her school bag, ready to take the trolley to school.

I took the doctor's advice seriously and began focusing on my own life. I sang as often as I could on weekends, and developed a repertoire of songs for different occasions, from children's and nonsense songs to songs of labor and political struggles. I performed at the Second Fret, a popular folk club in downtown Philadelphia. My brother did a drawing of me with my guitar for a promotional brochure designed and produced by a friend. I got bookings for a range of organizations, from the Rotary Club to the local YMCA, Vicki's elementary school and neighborhood events. In Bertolt Brecht's play, "A Man's a Man," in a local theater production, I acted and sang with guitar the part of Jenny Begbick.

I worked with several musician accompanists—Eliot Kenin, Billy Vanaver, and Mike Meeropol. Mike and his brother Robby had been adopted by Abel and Ann Meeropol after the political execution in 1953 of their parents, Julius & Ethel Rosenberg. Abel Meeropol had written the song "Strange Fruit" under the name Lewis Allen during the Cold War blacklisting of artists. Billie Holiday had made the song famous around the world and for all time.

Singing with Vicki

Vicki learned many of the songs and harmonies, and from the time she was six, often sang with me at bookings for schools and community groups around Philadelphia. A typical set included "Jenny Jenkins," "500 Miles," "The Ink Is Black," and "My Home's Across the Smoky Mountains." School kids loved seeing and hearing her singing out with her mother. We'd go to visit Jac and his kids and we'd all sing together in his VW bus on the way to their house. In 1962, at seven, Vicki Sue sang with a children's chorus in her first stage appearance in a benefit concert I produced with friends to raise money for Pete Seeger's First Amendment defense after he had been called to appear before the House Un-American Activities Committee. Singers, dancers, and musical groups contributed their talents to the concert, "For the Love of Pete," held at the University of Pennsylvania. And Vicki and I sang together at the First Philadelphia Folk Festival, Vicki standing on a chair to reach the microphone as we harmonized on "My Home's Across the Smoky Mountains" and "500 Miles."

Moving on

After 13 years as a member in cultural, trade union, and community clubs, I decided to leave the Communist Party. I was beginning to establish some priorities for myself, and Party membership was no longer one of them. I was no longer willing to keep the expected commitment in addition to being a mother, breadwinner, and woman seeking a career as a singer. Local Party leaders were friends who understood my decision. My experience in the Communist Party had provided a sense of community and structure, and an understanding of the wider world during crucial years of my young life.

William (Bill) Robinson and Jolly Smolens on their wedding day, July 7, 1951.

BIll Robinson in Riverside Park, Manhattan, 1955.

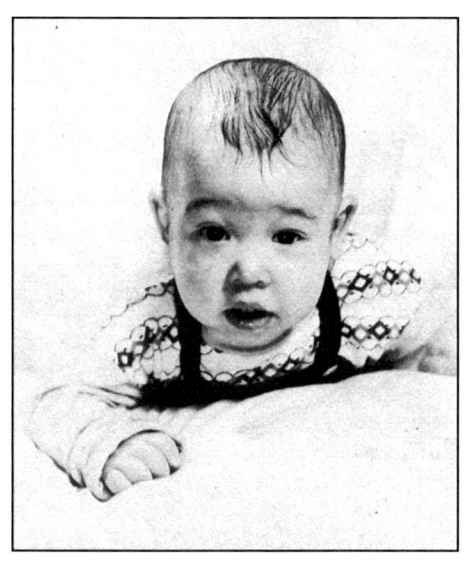

Vicki Sue Robinson, born May 31, 1954.

Jolly holds baby Vicki, with great-grandmother Cora and grandmother Amy looking on.

Vicki and kitty get acquainted.

Four generations in Arden. Seated, L-R: Mundi, Vicki, Amy, Teri, Rai (on Lloyd's lap), Cora. Behind them are Jac and Coby.

Vicki at 7 with friend Michele in Philadelphia.

> The Penn Folk Song Club and The Philadelphia Folk Workshop present
>
> **"FOR THE LOVE OF PETE"**
>
> A Concert in Tribute to Pete Seeger
>
> SATURDAY, MARCH 3, 1962 - 8 p.m.
>
> University Museum Auditorium
>
> program
>
> * TWO DANCES:
> Stop Now, It's Praying Time
> (composed and sung by Doug Quattlebaum)
> Strange Fruit
> (recording by Josh White) .... Audrey Bookspan
>
> Michael, Row the Boat Ashore
> Strangest Dream
> (accompanied by Jolly Robinson, guitar) .... Children's Chorus
>
> Pastures of Plenty
> This Land Is Your Land
> (accompanied by Bill Vanaver, guitar) .... Jolly Robinson
>
> * Rabbit in a Log
> Franklin D. Roosevelt's Back Again .... Old Towne Singers
>
> Ox Driver's Song
> Turtle Dove
> (accompanied by Dave Baskin, guitar) .... Kenny Snipes
>
> Chateau de Nouviel (Auvergne)
> Bara Loup Loup
> Si Mon Moine   (French) .... Suzanne Gross
>
> Talkin' Un-American Committee .... Eliot Kenin
>
> Sylvie
> No More Auction Block
> (accompanied by Eliot Kenin, guitar) .... Zarefa Storey
>
> I Promise the Lord
> What You Gonna Do When the World's on Fire? .... The Musicalaires
>
> INTERMISSION
> (15 minutes)
>
> *(Please note that these artists have been reversed)   (over)

> **"FOR THE LOVE OF PETE"**
>
> PART II
>
> Rawhide
> Dallas Rag .... Philadelphia Folk Workshop
>
> Talkin' Fallout Shelter (original composition)
> Passin' Through .... George Britton
>
> I'm A Vegetable
> Jovanno (Yugoslavian) .... Alix Dobkin
>
> I've Got a Home in That Rock
> Peace in the Valley
> No Hidin' Place Down Here .... Prof. Clarence Johnson
>   and Mabel Washington
>
> Russian Folk Dances .... Syd & Betty Dictor
>
> Micaballo (Chilean)
> Shir Hanoded (Hebrew) .... Elka Sylvern
>
> Hard Luck Blues
> Kansas City .... Doug Quattlebaum
>
> When the Saints Go Marching In .... Elmer Snowden with
>   Dixieland Combo
>   from "Club 13"
>
> Study War No More .... Ensemble
>
> Publicity: Barry Magarick, Chuck Romm, Manny Rubin, Karen Kramer, Kevin
>   Carroll, Lois Shipley, Lee Felsenstein, Howard Barkan
> Posters: Kenny Snipes, John Queen, Eliot Kenin
> Production: Nancy Miller, Jean Alexander, Peter Kuner, Willa Rose
> Arrangements: Andy Melamed, Peter Kuner, Barry Satlow, Bill Vanaver, Morton
>   Nahan, Lois Shipley, John Dyckman
> Advisors: Pete Welding, Kenneth Goldstein, Ivan Shaner, Harold Leventhal,
>   Herb Gart
>
> Produced by Jolly Robinson
> Directed by Ivan Shaner
>
> A heartfelt thank you to everyone who contributed time, money, talent, services and all the labors of love that brought this concert into being.

Program, "For the Love of Pete," a benefit concert for Pete Seeger's First Amendment defense after his indictment by HUAC. The event, involving a wide range of performers from the Philadelphia community, took place at the University of Pennsylvania in March, 1962.

Amy painted this 18x24"black-and-white image from a photograph of Jolly and Vicki singing together in Philadelphia when Vicki was 9.

Brochure promoting Jolly's singing career.
Below: Vicki sings with her Mom in close harmony.
Cover by Jac Smolens; layout & photos by Bill Hoffman Associates.

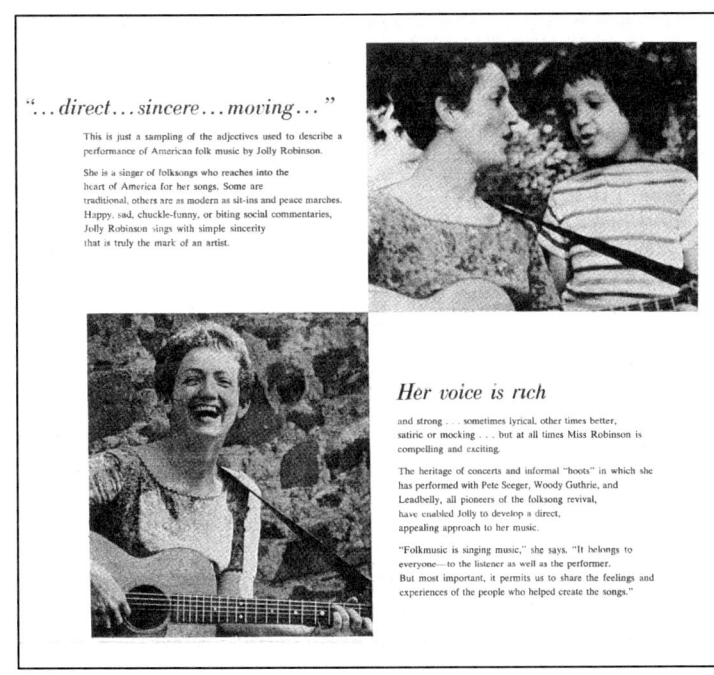

CHAPTER FOUR
Expanding Vistas, New Challenges

By 1964 I was trying to focus on a career in a more professional way, as a solo singer with guitar and repertoire. I'd been working full-time for 18 years and raising Vicki for the last ten. Through it all, I'd been singing for little or no pay for political causes, unions, and community organizations. Songs chosen to fit specific themes and occasions helped bring people together around important issues and added a lively dimension to events dominated by speakers. Now, in the 60s, the "folk song revival" was exploding, with performers becoming known for songs and styles identified with them—women as well as men. For the first time, I wanted to sing songs of my choice as Jolly Robinson, in venues not limited to political issues and themes.

When I wrote to Pete Seeger asking for advice about getting bookings, he answered that there was no easy road, and Toshi added bluntly that my first responsibility was to my daughter—after all, she said, Pete had a wife to support his career. No surprise that prior to the 1960s, most of my role models had been male singers whose voices were heard and careers made possible because of women who were caring for the kids and holding down the home front.

Leon Bibb was a fine singer I had met through People's Songs, a trained and versatile artist whose range included musical theater and concert performance. When he came to Philadelphia to perform, I told him of my desire to develop my career. As I was not a songwriter, he advised me to choose five favorite songs as the basis of my repertoire and build on that. Smaller is better, he said. Do a limited program well and become identified with it. This was wise advice I could act on.

A tough decision

In her tenth year, Vicki's school and friends and life were in Powelton Village. She stayed with a neighbor's kids two blocks from home till I came for her after work. In the years after Bill left, her life had become more stable.

On holiday weekends we would go by train to visit Jac and his growing family in rural Pennsylvania or Maryland. My job with the Glass Bottle Blowers Association, though hardly memorable, was secure. But I felt that I needed to be in New York City to pursue a career as a folksinger. New York was the hub of music and the arts, with its potential for growth in the area of my interests and connections. Besides, it was only 90 miles away, and I had lived there before.

Naturally there was conflict. Wasn't it selfish of me and harmful to Vicki to tear her away from her friends and connections? Could I find a decent place to live, and how would my child make the transition to a new school and a new life in a strange city? Amy, I knew, would be dead set against this move to the big city I had left because of a failed marriage a few years before. But a good friend counseled that I needed to do what was right for me and have faith that when Vicki was older she would make her own decisions. Besides, Vicki had already shown signs of becoming a singer in her own right, and New York would be the place for her, too. (She later spoke of New York as her home and seldom mentioned Philadelphia.)

The moth to the flame

In February 1964 I took the leap. Through music connections, I found a job with Al Grossman, personal manager of Bob Dylan, Peter, Paul & Mary, Odetta, Ian & Sylvia, and other folksingers, and arranged to stay with my friend Anne Quashen while I looked for an apartment. Vicki remained in Philadelphia with a family in their home until school was out in June. I visited on weekends, and we celebrated her 10th birthday in Powelton Village with our friends. In June I brought her to the apartment I had found on West 82nd Street. (Al Grossman had cosigned the lease when the landlord refused to rent to a single woman with a child.) That summer, while I held down the job, Vicki spent two weeks at a camp and stayed another two weeks with Amy in upstate New York. On Labor Day weekend, we went to visit Jac's family in Maryland. There were no public child care programs then, and parents were on their own if they had to work to support their children. Before the school term began, I made plans for after-school care for my 10-year-old daughter.

In September, Vicki entered fifth grade at P.S. 41, the public school within walking distance from our apartment. She went home with a classmate and I came for her after work and met some of the mothers of her classmates. The next year we arranged that she could let herself into our apartment, with orders to lock the door and not let anyone in. I felt terrible about being powerless to change the situation for my "latch-key child." (Years later she told me that she would tiptoe past the door and not flush the toilet so no one would know she was there.) Juggling work and parenting were primary. My career plans were dispensable, put on hold. "Role juggler" became my theme.

Poems of loneliness

I started writing poems and prose late at night after Vicki was in bed. The writing erupted from feelings of alienation, loneliness, starting over again in New York, trying to promote my career while working every weekday with sole responsibility for raising my child. I wrote about the "still, small voice" yearning to be heard, be visible, show that I was somebody besides an adjunct to a boss, a movement, a role. I wrote, too, of the pain of seeing my daughter go off to camp for two weeks the same summer I had brought her there. I felt suspended somewhere between dream and reality. I'm here, alone, where is everybody? Why are they out there doing great things while time is going by and I'm sitting here? I had already been "out there," engaged, involved, on the move, singing; but now I was trapped, unable to change my situation, with no one to share parenting. I went to work by day, but that wasn't who I was, and I didn't know how to get to who I was. Many poems and writings over the years have been about the difficulty of "getting to it," to my real work.

My first poems were short, hesitant, as if something might interrupt them mid-thought—the external demands and frequent dislocations of my reality. They were about transience, distrust, disbelief, seizing the beauty of the moment in the knowledge that it would not last, would be "gone with the world of everyday." Poems of loneliness, longing, grasping the "fleeting moment," wondering what tomorrow would bring. It was many years before I thought of myself as "a poet." Writing was part of my living process; it helped me get a firmer grasp on my life and its elusive meaning.

Fragments

Scattered fragments
pieces of me
all over the city

I see them indelibly etched
in a corner
an intersection
a street light
blending into rainy pavement
a sound from a jukebox

Bridges
between past
and today.

Nostalgia

Nostalgia
expansion of soft
rain-threatening
grey, moody
swift-changing, fleeting
clouds

A jazz beat
wood on brass
bittersweet horn
blowing terrible, beautiful
memories
of other times. . .far away

Making yesterday one
inextricably
painfully
bound up
with today.

Gaslight Café

Everyone has a story.

Every singer has a soul
    brimming
        full to overflowing.

To find yourself can take a lifetime.
Becoming is all.

    When Al Grossman told me after four months that things weren't working out; I was being "too friendly with the artists," it turned out for the best. My magazine publishing experience won me a good job at Grosset & Dunlap Books, an old, established publishing firm at 51 Madison Avenue. (Remember the *Nancy Drew* and *Hardy Boys* series?) The next four years as secretary to the Editor-in-Chief gave me valuable experience in editing and publishing to augment what I had learned in magazine publishing. The managing editor assigned some books to me to review, and I wrote brief summaries that helped develop my editing and writing skills.

Juggling act

Through it all, I managed to get bookings and to sing at events here and there, and found some good musicians to accompany me on second guitar. I made an audition tape with Eliot Kenin, who had helped produce the benefit concert for Pete Seeger in Philadelphia. I rehearsed and performed with Mike Meeropol, and with Marshall Freedland, a fine banjo picker and guitarist. In 1965, I sang in a Tribute to Woody Guthrie at Town Hall with Pete Seeger, Odetta, Jack Elliot and others. Woody sat in the balcony with his family, and my daughter and my mother were in the audience. It was an unforgettable experience, as I sang solo and in combination with folksingers I had admired for decades.

For awhile during the 60s I took voice lessons to increase my range and clarity. At a Broadside Hoot in the Village billed as a topical song workshop, I was on the program with Pete Seeger, Alex Dobkin, Phil Ochs, Janis Ian, Julius Lester, Carolyn Hester, Irma Jurist, Peter Lafarge, and Pat Sky. I sang Malvina Reynolds's song, "What Have They Done to the Rain?" Soon after the show, Pete wrote bluntly, "Get rid of that voice teacher! I liked your voice better when it had that hard, flat sound." I kept up the lessons anyway.

At a "Folk Music at the [Village] Gate" benefit for unemployed Kentucky miners, I sang in the company of Bob Gibson, Tom Paxton, Brother John Sellers, Phil Ochs, comedian Flip Wilson, Jim & Jean, Jesse Colin Young, Pat Sky, and Eliot Kenin. There were bookings at smaller venues, and sometimes Vicki sang with me in duet or solo, gaining experience and recognition for her strong, true voice.

After one performance in the Village, the fine Martin guitar I had bought in 1945 was stolen from the back seat of a friend's car. My boss at Grosset & Dunlap said he was tired of seeing me looking as if I had lost my best friend, and asked how much another guitar would cost. Through Fretted Instruments, part of Izzy Young's Folklore Center in the Village, I located a 1938 Martin guitar made of koa wood being rebuilt from a Hawaiian guitar, priced at $125. My boss paid for it, and then invited me to visit him in Connecticut. A payback for his generous offer of help? After he was fired for reasons I never knew, the boss who replaced him asked me to put drops in his eyes and take his trousers to be pressed. I wondered what his wife's duties were.

Turning points at 40

In 1967 I fell in love with a Scotsman who ran an Irish bar. That Christmas he gave Vicki her first guitar. After we'd been going together for nearly a year, he announced that he had to go to Scotland to take care of his ailing father. As days and weeks went by with no word, I was heartbroken and disconsolate, facing the likelihood that he would not return. I had grown increasingly restless and dissatisfied with my work scene, frustrated about my career plans, and weary of holding everything together. I decided to quit the job, go to London for three weeks, and figure out next steps when I returned. Vicki would stay with my mother in Connecticut while I was gone. In June 1968, I said goodbye to Grosset & Dunlap, collected $1500 in accrued profit-sharing, and flew to London on my first real vacation and trip abroad.

From a small hotel in South Kensington near Chelsea I got acquainted with London by foot, bus, taxicab, and Underground. I looked up my old friend Tom Paley, who was living in London, and he introduced me to British beer and ale at local pubs. I made the rounds of the burgeoning folk music clubs and took a train to the Cambridge Folk Festival, featuring Odetta and Tom Rush among its roster of performers. In a last-ditch attempt to find my lost lover, I located his sister in a London suburb. She said, "Oh, forget about Tommy—he's a loser." So I closed the book on that dead-end affair and went back to New York, overjoyed to see Vicki and Amy and embark on the next unknown chapter of my life.

Vicki had made friends among the kids at her public school, and several remained close friends all her life. After school, all the kids hung out in Central Park around the big fountain, not far from the meadow where huge concerts and rallies were held. In their early teens, many smoked marijuana and experimented with harder drugs, and Vicki was no exception. It was 1968, the year of "The Summer of Love" in San Francisco. When she was 14, I took her with her boyfriend Marty to Phoenix House to check out the youth drug rehab program there, but they never went back. (Years later, she told me she had wanted to return but Marty refused, so that ended that.) Two years later she had a close call with LSD—an "acid trip"—that included lashing out at me and trying to jump out the apartment window. Luckily I was able to get her to a doctor in time. She was given a sedative and slept for 24 hours.

Shaken by the challenges of my life, I got myself into therapy with a woman I felt comfortable with, and continued to see her weekly until she stopped practicing to enter specialized training. I continued to work with therapists, when I could afford it, in an ongoing effort to learn what the forces were that drove me to both self-destructive and self-affirming behavior—what made me tick.

Breaking new ground

I returned from England in 1968 determined to find ways to do work of my choosing and stop working as a secretary. The anti-Vietnam War movement was in full swing, the Civil Rights Movement was making gains, and the counter-culture was exploding everywhere. A man I liked a lot left for the "Summer of Love" and that was the last I saw of him. Through the 60s I rejected proposals of marriage from three men—all on the rebound from marriages—because I was not attracted to them or the wife they wanted me to be. I could not leave my child and my job to go south on Freedom Rides, but I participated in anti-war marches, sang here and there, and in 1969 became involved in the new Women's Liberation Movement. A consciousness-raising group and books by feminist writers gave me new insights, and active participation in the movement affirmed my lifelong feelings about the roles girls and women are expected to serve.

While working at temporary jobs in publishing, I enrolled in two evening classes, Art History and Sociology, at Columbia University's extension program. I answered a newspaper ad placed by Alan Lomax for office assistance on a project funded by Columbia's anthropology department. Lomax had been instrumental in documenting, recording, and promoting American folk music since the 1930s and had been on the People's Songs board of directors. With a professional choreographer, he was doing a cross-cultural study called Choreometrics on dance and movement styles around the world, showing how they were related to indigenous work and ritual. For six months I typed research studies and handled office duties in his West 92nd Street office within walking distance from my apartment. Lomax listened to my audition tapes and placed my musical roots in Baltimore—not far from Arden, Delaware!

College at 41

Alan Lomax encouraged me to take college seriously and get into a degree program, stressing that a liberal arts education was part of my cultural heritage. Knowing of my background and participation in folk music, he urged me to talk to Margaret Mead about taking her course on Culture and Communication. This was another landmark piece of advice, and I acted on it. I wrote a biographical summary, arranged an interview with Dr. Mead, applied to Columbia University, and in 1970 started my BA degree program in a graduate-level course in Anthropology.

The Culture and Communication course was followed by a semester in Anthropology Field Methods. Both classes required teamwork in projects originated by the students under minimal supervision by Dr. Mead. I plunged in with whole heart and mind, working with a small group of classmates to design and carry out fieldwork in Manhattan that involved observation and note-taking, photography and filmmaking, all on location. The first project took place in a classroom setting with high school students, in which we showed a documentary film about the effects of a huge dam project on the lives of people in upstate New York, and then recorded the students' responses. The second project centered around the lives of two artists and their child in an industrial loft, in which we photographed, filmed, recorded and took notes on "a day in the life." We reported periodically to Dr. Mead, who gave us critiques and encouragement. I loved every minute of it, and received A's in both courses. The single most important lesson I learned about research methods from Margaret Mead was her strong insistence that all members of a research or work team must have the same information at each step of a project.

A man in my life

On a Saturday in early May 1969, I dropped in at St. Adrian's, a lively bar in lower Manhattan frequented by an eclectic mix of artists and working people where I knew the bartender and enjoyed the late afternoon scene. I struck up a conversation with an artist named Bob Bolles, who invited me to his place for dinner and said he'd be back after he did some shopping. When a young man took the bar stool next to mine, the bartender introduced me to Tom Schultz, a painter who was no stranger to the bar. We talked, one thing led to another, we went to a Village restaurant for dinner, and spent the night together. It turned out that Tom and Bob Bolles were good friends.

Tom had moved to New York City from Colorado Springs when he was 20. A high school art teacher opened many doors, and a well-known painter, Charles Bunnell, had encouraged him to continue painting. After an art exhibit in Colorado Springs, Bunnell had advised Tom, "You're wasting your time here, kid. Go to New York!" On arriving in Manhattan in 1959, at the height of the Abstract Expressionist period, he was given a show in a small gallery and quickly became immersed in the art scene downtown, where the 10th Street Co-op Galleries flourished. The artists and their followers hung out at the Cedar Tavern, where he met Willem deKooning, Franz Kline, Herman Cherry, Robert Goodnough, and many others. He supported himself by stretching canvases for artists and doing house painting and carpentry jobs.

We began seeing each other often, making the rounds of Manhattan bars and restaurants, going to art openings, and renting bicycles to explore Manhattan. After a few months, Tom gave up his Delancey Street studio and we began living together in my 82nd Street apartment. Vicki was hostile at first, naturally skeptical about this new man in her mother's life. On Memorial Day weekend—also her 15th birthday—the three of us went by train to see Jac and his kids on the Eastern Shore of Maryland. Tom met my family, and little by little, Vicki began to accept that he was going to be in my life.

That summer, Vicki announced that she was going to the Woodstock Festival with friends. I was opposed to the idea, but she was too old for camp and I did not have an alternative plan, so I arranged for her to bunk with a family friend in Woodstock. She assured me she would call from there, but when I had no word for two days, I phoned and learned that she had checked in but had left to stay with a commune. She did call, saying she had a great time serving food at the festival, and announcing that she and friends were going to hitchhike to the Newport Folk Festival and she'd be home after that! Some coming-of-age teen-age ritual that summer was!

Beginnings and endings

In one of the classes at Columbia I had met Gail Sheehy, a writer with *New York Magazine,* who asked me to work as her assistant two days a week. She also referred me to Gloria Steinem, another writer who needed someone to assist her two days a week from her home office. Freed at last from full-time employment, I began seeking editorial and proofreading work for the fifth day, and often weekends.

The course of events in the early 70s is impossible to track clearly. The pieces of my life were overlapping, beginning and ending, interacting and feeding each other. There were still the roles to juggle—mother, breadwinner, student, woman seeking her true calling. But now each role broadened and took new forms. I was mother to a child fast becoming an adult. Vicki experimented with living situations, sharing apartments with friends from high school and show business. From 17 on, she was in and out of the 82nd Street apartment until she was permanently living on her own. I can never forget her instruction: "Mom, I want you to always keep a bed for me."

Pieces together

putting the pieces together
that's what it's all about

my whole life
a puzzle
a search
a journey
toward wholeness

those years in Philadelphia
the hard-edge years
the years of black and red
of drinking & defying
      but also
wistful longing
looking up from down
through the trees to the sky

always above me
out there somewhere
green and yellow, beckoning
from years to come

all the while knowing
in my spirit   body   soul
that what I was seeking
was here inside
insisting on being heard
sometimes whispering
sometimes screaming

relentlessly driving me
to pay attention
heed the voice
follow the signs
along the way
on this journey
this work in progress

putting the pieces
together.

New vistas

Working for Gloria Steinem in 1971, I met women who were forming the Women's Political Caucus, Women's Action Alliance, and what would become *Ms. Magazine*. I found that while I agreed wholeheartedly with the push for women's and racial equality in higher education, the professions, the government, and the home, there was little attention given to the realities working-class women faced in their daily lives—my own reality as a mother who had worked to support myself and my child while seeking "my real work." After reading a proposal for one of the new women's organizations, I told Gloria that I did not see myself reflected as a single working mother. If it did not speak to my life, I reasoned, it also left out a lot of other women.

Gloria referred me to an executive at the John Hay Whitney Foundation, and I wrote a proposal describing the need for research on low-income, working women. I succeeded in getting funding for an independent research project I would design and conduct with two women I knew on access to higher education for low-income women. Called "Project Second Start" and based at Brooklyn College, the year-long study involved interviewing 50 students who were low-income mothers in three adult degree programs established during the 1960s "War on Poverty." As a 43-year-old working mother enrolled in one of those evening programs while conducting the study during the day, I was a peer of these women. The study group also interviewed teachers and high-level administrators. We were paid monthly, a welcome development in my new self-employed situation.

The three of us met and strategized regularly, divided up the interviews, conducted them with tape recorders, wrote up our findings, and reported monthly to each other and the foundation. In 1972 we wrote a 308-page report that was published, promoted, and distributed nationally by the Whitney Foundation. Five years later, we received a small grant to do a follow-up study with some of the women to see how their lives had changed.

Being in close contact with Gloria and being part of the new Women's Movement was energizing and helped me understand my feelings, my decisions, my life. With other women, I helped choose the name *"Ms."* for the new feminist magazine. After its founding, I worked in the office part-time, answering Gloria's mail to earn some regular income. As a freelance photographer, I photographed women picketing in front of *The New York Times*. One of the signs read, "Our Mrs. or Miss-ness is nobody's business."

The Women's Movement affirmed things I had always felt and acted on alone, and now there was a sisterhood that spoke publicly about violence against women, women's rights in marriage, the home, the workplace, in politics and all walks of life. I was personally acquainted with the danger to women's lives of illegal abortions, and I celebrated the victory of Roe v Wade with millions of women across the country. I could relate personally to the growing consciousness about women's domestic work as valuable unpaid labor, and to the necessity for many women, like myself, to work both on the home front and at jobs to support themselves and their children. The slogan "THE PERSONAL IS POLITICAL" spoke for me. It enabled me to understand the experiences I had had in many roles—as single woman, wife, mother, house worker, wage earner, political activist.

After completing Dr. Mead's courses at Columbia, I had transferred my degree program to City University of New York (CUNY) and plunged into a 12-credit-a-semester, evening course in Humanities in the Special BA Degree Program at Brooklyn College. I traveled by subway to classes in Flatbush, often studying standing up (a "strap-hanger") after working by day on Project Second Start. The class read and discussed world literature, made oral presentations, and wrote papers on topics of our choice—three papers the first semester and a term paper the second semester. My term paper was "Morality and Change: The Theater of Berthold Brecht." The three shorter papers were: "The Status of Women in Homeric Greece," "The Folk Process: The Oral Tradition in Medieval Music," and "Praise of Folly" on Erasmus's "social pamphlet" on Humanist values during the 16th century Renaissance. It was surely one of the most challenging years of my life—conducting a research study by day, attending classes two nights a week, reading, researching, and writing papers on subjects of my choice.

The next year, as part of the CUNY BA program, I took classes in film history and filmmaking at Hunter College. As a class project, I made a 12-minute silent film of Vicki with cast members in a dressing room backstage in "Jesus Christ, Superstar." The teacher wrote this comment about "The Understudy":

"Jolly Robinson

The most successful documentary, not because of its careful treatment and thorough reporting, but because you were able to infuse a little bit of the excitement and love of the filmmaker into the subject. A good feeling for intimacy and a good eye for details made 'The Understudy' a happy event, a celebration."

The Soviet Union up close

In 1971 the big "thaw" in superpower relations was finally opening the door for citizens of other countries to travel inside the Soviet Union. During the spring semester with Margaret Mead, I heard about a summer tour to the Soviet Union being conducted by the Citizens' Exchange Corps. The organization's purpose was to organize tour groups of 40 Americans and arrange "counterpart visits" to facilitate information and understanding between citizens of both countries. Gail Sheehy and I both signed up for a month-long trip that included stays in Moscow, Leningrad, and Kiev, as well as three Central Asian cities. I figured it was now or never for such an ambitious endeavor. I borrowed $1000 for the trip, left Vicki and Tom in the apartment to look after each other, and took off for the longest adventure away from home. The plane made stops in London, Amsterdam, and Helsinki before flying to Moscow.

Gail and I shared hotel rooms in all three cities and went with different groups to meet with people according to our professional interests. Not being sure what my profession was, I chose to go with a small group to visit a violinist in her Moscow apartment. She served us potato soup, and there was vodka wherever we went! There were about six interpreters with the delegation of 40, so at times we walked in small groups or alone without interpreters. I was fired up about photographing everywhere we went and brought home a slide documentary of the tour. We were taken to outdoor amusement parks, the Moscow Ballet, and to a meet with a group of sociologists. Everywhere we saw people reading the newspapers posted daily on the huge outdoor kiosks.

Stressed by the long flight and constant adjustment to unfamiliar conditions, my neck and back were stiff and painful, and I went to a free hospital clinic to get some relief. Imagine my dismay when the female doctor advised me to take two aspirin and get some rest! I learned that chiropractic was not a medical option in the USSR; also that there were more women than men doctors largely because of the huge losses of World War II.

In Leningrad I went with a small group to the studio of an abstract painter whose work was not approved by the State. He survived by cosigning the large outdoor murals made by his wife, whose work was politically acceptable! He told of selling some of his work abroad, and a member of our tour group arranged to buy one of his paintings and take the rolled-up canvas with her on the plane. Sure enough, it was confiscated at the airport, creating an incident that held up our delegation. I was not happy that she would take it on herself to test the still-fragile détente and jeopardize the goodwill mission of our group in the process.

In Kiev I looked for signs of anti-Semitism, as my Jewish grandparents had emigrated from Ukraine. When we did meet some Jews, I sensed a reluctance to speak about their experience. In Kiev I had a claustrophobic experience in being escorted with a group through a historical catacomb with a single-file tunnel too narrow to turn around in, and a rock ceiling about an inch overhead! I nearly panicked and was relieved to see the daylight again.

While we were in Kiev we learned that the fourth week of the tour had been canceled because travel and hotel arrangements had not worked out. It seems the logistics of booking travel and lodging in far-flung areas of the USSR was far more difficult than visiting the major cities in Russia and Ukraine. As always after being away from home, I returned exhausted, and overjoyed to be reunited with Vicki and Tom in New York.

The end of a life

After divorcing Amy, Henry had remarried Mary, who worked in his real estate office. He and Mary had adopted a child named Jonny, who was cared for by Shirley, a younger woman, during the day. Not long after Mary tragically committed suicide, Henry married Shirley and they had a son, Jamie, together. With little or no relationship with Henry after I returned to New York in 1964, I hardly got to know my two half-brothers.

I had seldom seen Henry after his second marriage. Once in the 60s I had convinced him to come with Shirley to a reunion gathering at Jac's workshop, Farmer's Exchange, in rural Pennsylvania. I didn't see my father again until 1971, when I returned to New York from the Soviet Union to learn that he had had a severe stroke and was in intensive care. Tom, who had never met my father, went with me to see him in the hospital, and we stayed overnight in the house in Upper Darby, with all its unhappy memories. The stroke had partially paralyzed Henry, and despite attempts at rehabilitation in a nursing home, he died within the year. His business partners handled all the details and personal affairs, keeping me informed by mail. His assets, including the house, were divided among his debtors and his two young children. Jac and I each received a small check.

Twenty-two years later the words that I could not have spoken or written earlier came to me in the form of this farewell to my father.

I never said goodbye . . .

Henry, my father, I miss you. I never got to say a proper goodbye after you had a stroke and I saw you in the hospital with tubes and attachments, unable to speak. That was the last time I saw you ever.

Others presided over your last rites—your office assistant, your third wife Shirley, your lawyer. People unrelated to our family were with you as you made your wishes known about how your estate would be distributed and all the end-of-life matters you handled as efficiently as you ran your business seven days a week.

I loved you so much—you gave me a clear sense of who I was. We were the passionate ones—I inherited your earthiness, your depth of feeling, your quick wit, sarcasm and repartee, your brooding moods and gloomy outlook, your outbursts of laughter or anger, followed suddenly by a need to retreat behind your newspaper and be alone. Your sensuality, especially the sense of touch—fondling a smooth cane you had whittled and sanded and oiled to accompany your walk; sanding and caressing the massive oak table you loved to preside over.

First providing, then presiding over the table groaning with Thanksgiving turkey and plenty of food, surrounded by relatives and friends, the more the merrier. The knife-sharpening ritual and your insistence that guests make their preferences known, the utter delight in enjoying the food and drink you didn't have when you were growing up. You worked hard to bring bounty to the big oak table, to those gathered around it.

I miss you, Henry. It's been twenty-two years since your death when I was forty-four. We hadn't seen a lot of each other after I left home at twenty; there had been estrangement and pain between us. The love for you that I grew up with was mixed with fear and anger in my teenage years. I felt let down and betrayed at 18 because I had planned and longed to go to college and you insisted "you'll learn to make a living." Our contact was mostly around my recurring needs for financial help and a home to come to after you married again and my mother left for New England with her new husband.

You and Mary visited me once in NYC after my marriage to Bill. As always you were the host and treated us to a sumptuous meal at a Village restaurant. Five years later you helped by paying for my divorce and part of my rent in Philadelphia when Vicki was 19 months old. Once you asked if I had thought of giving her up for adoption.

But still I miss you. I miss all the things we didn't get to say to each other that would be so much easier now. Ironic about the passage of time and the wisdom that only years can bring. The last time I saw you socially was when *you came to a reunion party I planned at Jac's studio in West Chester, and you got so drunk that we helped you into your car and Shirley drove you home.*

I forgive you now for not being there in the ways that were most important to a girl growing up, looking to her father for a masculine role model in her adult life. If only you could have lived long enough for real communication and sharing some of the things I've come to know I got from you—passion for life and love and laughter, depth of feeling, a keen sense of
humor that came from your Jewish working class origins, a love of pleasure and beauty, compassion for ordinary people, a hunger for knowledge.

Rest well, my father, and know I love you.
October 1994

Comings and goings

Somewhere between 1971 and 1972, with Vicki's comings and goings and the demands of my freelance work, studies, creative projects, and paying the bills, the pressures mounted. Carpentry work and pay were slow to nonexistent for Tom during that recession period. He was depressed, drinking daily, and not carrying his share. I needed more space and fewer distractions, and I insisted he find a place of his own. It turned out to be a good move for both of us, and we got along better living separately. We signed up for a class in Marx's *Das Capital,* taught by the director of the Marxist Education Collective. We went to anti-war demonstrations in New York and Washington, and marched, single file, through SoHo (South of Houston) protesting the invasion of Cambodia. We participated in the struggle of working artists being denied live/work space in vacated industrial buildings, chanting "SoHo sucks! Bring back the trucks!" The artists laid the groundwork for a gentrified SoHo that artists could not afford to live in.

In 1973 we drove up the Atlantic coast to Maine, and across Maine to New Hampshire and Vermont, on a two-week trip. Tom got to go fishing twice, and I photographed people and places along the way. I still have the $6 wooden rocking chair that came home with us in the back seat of the rented car. We drove to the top of Mount Washington, the highest peak in New Hampshire's White Mountains, and witnessed the falls that flowed over smooth, red rocks at Flume Gorge.

That winter I took a break from work and responsibilities, and with some of the money Henry had left me, Tom and I flew to St. Thomas for a two-week winter vacation in the Virgin Islands. It was the most idyllic time away I have ever known—a restful contrast to the stressful trips to England and the USSR. We saw every inch of that island, its beaches and small-town ambience, its sun and hills and people. We checked in at a small beach hotel, and then an old hotel in the center of town. Tom drove our little car—on the left side, as in British territories—and I photographed everything in color for a slide show.

Vicki was trying her wings in the singing career that was clearly her calling. At the urging of Robert Greenwald, her high school teacher who later became a famous film producer, she auditioned and was hired to sing in the chorus of "Hair" on Broadway. (She had to get my signed permission to appear in the nude scene.) She sang with an interracial chorus that visited public schools. She played in an off-Broadway show with a young Richard Gere. She went to Japan on a two-month tour with a rock band. At 19, she was in the chorus and understudied the part of Mary in "Jesus Christ, Superstar" on Broadway.

Theater, drama, and tragedy

In early 1975, Bill Robinson returned to New York from Boston, where he'd lived since leaving Philadelphia. He made contact with Vicki, they visited once or twice, and he came to see her in "Superstar." Bill applauded and cheered loudly from the audience while she was onstage. She was humiliated as cast members asked, "Who is that man?" Here was her father—her role model as an actor—proud of his daughter but making a fool of himself. Painful as that experience was for Vicki, it was overshadowed by Bill's death, just as her career was about to take off in a big way.

One day a police officer knocked on my door, asking if I was Mrs. Jolly Robinson and would I come to the morgue to identify Bill's body. In shock, Vicki, Tom and I made the trip together, and I accompanied the officer downstairs to the morgue. Poems I wrote afterwards say it better than I can 30 years later. Bill had died alone in his hotel room at 50. He had returned to New York after a 13-year absence, hoping to make a new start. Instead, he had come to an abrupt and early end. All they would say about the diagnosis, when I asked, was "fatty liver." I knew that he had been dealing with diabetes, on top of a lifetime of alcohol and drugs. Now he could no longer embarrass or disappoint his only daughter—nor could he be the father she had longed for.

Nothing of Value

So this is how it ends.
Blackout on the floor of a hotel room
Alone.
Found by strangers.

"Time of death unknown."

Surrounded by the identifying documents of a lifetime.
Hospital I.D. bracelet, Navy discharge papers, prescription drugs (this time),
AA literature, religious words-to-live-by
And more.
Clippings, letters, pictures of times gone and ties broken,
Prison poems of repentance.

"Who do we notify?" the cops ask each other.

So this is how it ends.
An ear, an eye (was it pain?), discolored flesh (he looked so small),
All I could see of a body sheathed in a shroud on a cold morgue table.
I looked and turned away, stumbled up the stairs.
"He's not in pain any more," I cried to our daughter.

So this is how it ends.
He was trying to renew, revive, put back together, mend the lost years,
The sickness, the agony, the abuse.
Trying to replace suffering with recovery.
Hold on to hope.

"Nothing of value," the cops reported, was found in the room.

Nothing but the story of his life.

    I organized an informal memorial service at the Bronx home of one of Bill's sisters, attended by all his living family. It was so important for Vicki to be able to say farewell to the father she had known only for brief periods of her 20-year life. Awhile later, we took Bill's ashes out on the Staten Island Ferry, as he had wished, and Vicki scattered them to the wind and water.

    Not long after Bill's death, I photographed Vicki at Tom's studio as part of a portrait class I was taking. That same year she signed a contract with RCA Records, and I photographed her debut at the RCA studios. So much was happening so fast, in such a short time.

One song in Vicki's first RCA album took off at dance clubs and hit the charts within days of the record's release. "Turn the Beat Around" (written by the Jackson brothers) became the keynote song of the Disco explosion and remained #1 on the charts for 21 weeks. Walking home from my part-time job on Central Park West, I would hear Vicki's live-wire voice in this irresistible dance tune coming from taxicabs and apartment windows. Could it be my little girl that everybody in the world was listening to? Barely 21, she began touring with a six-piece band and three back-up singers, playing big clubs, concerts, and dance halls from New York to California. In addition to her paid gigs, Vicki appeared in many benefits to combat AIDS, inspired by the huge gay crowd in the disco clubs that put her and her songs on the map.

Photography—my true calling?

Tom had seen the photographs I'd taken with a little Brownie camera on my lunch hours, and on our first Christmas together he gave me a 35mm Nikko mat camera. It opened up a whole new visual world of creative challenge. I lost no time in learning how to use it and began photographing people and places all over New York. I took classes in photography basics and portraiture. I learned how to print my black and white photographs in a darkroom rented from Richard Borst at his basement studio in the Village. When Vicki moved out of the apartment in the mid-70s, Tom, the skilled carpenter, made a custom darkroom in her former bedroom so I could do my printing and enlarging at home.

With 24 academic credits and 18 credits for life experience (including Project Second Start and my film) amounting to half a BA degree, I made a decision to drop the degree program in favor of working at photography—both as freelance journalism and art. It was a toss-up between two more years of college while trying to pay the rent, and taking a gamble on photography as a livelihood. I had found photography, and this was what I wanted to focus on for the rest of my life. Photography gave me a way to capture what I saw, what was important to me, and to communicate it visually to others. I was strongly drawn to filmmaking as well, and got as far as drafting scripts for films I wanted to make and inquiring about funding. But the basic dilemma of how to pay the rent while doing the research and fundraising needed to make a film confronted me once again. I decided to focus on still photography.

I developed contacts for work as a photojournalist covering labor and women's movement events. *The New York Times, New York Magazine, Ms. Magazine* and other publications published some of my photographs.

McGraw-Hill Books published two series of photos—one on women workers in nontraditional occupations, one on multigenerational families—as educational materials for classrooms. At times I found it necessary to supplement the unsteady income from photography with typing and proofreading work. At one point I found myself typing 3x5 cards for an hourly fee. I quickly discovered that self-employment is often mixed with under-employment and unemployment, there's no easy road when you're doing your "real work," and the elation it brings is usually short-lived.

Fleeting Moments

Such a sadness, a beauty,
bittersweet longing
for a time, a place that once was
      (never)
exquisite moments I knew
      (or did I dream them?)
precious jewels of time
stolen from relentless reality...

They were of a quality
like the flare of light
before dying,
like a brief second of calm
amid surrounding storm...

Such essence of life that I knew
I couldn't trust them—
they'd be gone with the morning,
with return to the world of everyday.

Just the same, I hunger
for those moments
snatched from the everyday.

I will recreate them—
or make new ones
out of spider webs
and rainbows.

Side by side with photojournalism was the "Labor Songs as History" course I developed, illustrating labor history through live and recorded songs, with emphasis on working women. Two colleges were interested in my course proposal, but during the recession of 1971-72 it was rejected in favor of more basic classes. I adapted the course and taught it as a one-time class presentation to organizations like the Coalition for Labor Union Women (CLUW), New York State School of Industrial and Labor Relations (NYSSILR), AFSCME District Council 37, and women's and labor studies programs. It took me as far afield as colleges in New Jersey, Rhode Island, and Massachusetts. In 1975 I photographed the First International Women's Day March in New York for four women's and labor organizations. I took photos along the entire route along from 5th Avenue & 42nd Street to Union Square, scene of many previous marches and rallies. In 1977, 24 of my photographs from this historic occasion were shown at the International Women's Conference held in Houston.

My freelance photos were published in newspapers, magazines, and books; other work was exhibited by galleries, libraries, museums and public places, culminating in a month-long show at the Work of Art Gallery in Brooklyn Heights.

The Work of Art show, called "City and Country Impressions," was a landmark event, a collaboration between my brother and me. Jac brought his organic, "tree-form" sculptured wood pieces from Maryland to occupy the space, while my black-and-white urban photographs covered the walls. I publicized the month-long show in New York media, and it was well-attended and reviewed. Amy, not wanting to miss this rare exhibit by both her children, came from Arden to the "big city" for the opening.

In 1975, in the midst of preparing this large exhibit, I wrote a prose piece expressing my frustration with the contradictions inherent in working as a photographer, with its costly equipment and materials but no money to underwrite the business. I was good at taking risks and trying new ventures, and working hard to produce results. What was lacking was capital to keep me going between the erratic checks that came in.

What price photography?
A prose poem

Of course—that's it.
I'm not supposed to do it. Photography?
My own thing? MY work?

As I sit typing 3x5 cards and address lists I think of the contradiction:

I'm working for $5 an hour at typing so that I can pay the landlord. After that I borrow money and take money from Tom's labor and live on credit (from the "old days" when I had a steady office job I hated) so I can try to do photography which I can't afford, so I have to return to typing 3x5 cards.

Where am I to get money—capital—to invest in the tools and materials and skills I need to call myself a photographer? Oh, maybe I am a photographer, but TO DO PHOTOGRAPHY? TO MAKE A LIVING AT PHOTOGRAPHY? That's a horse of an entirely different color.

The names and addresses go on, and on, and on. I find myself envying the women whose names are on the cards because at least they aren't typing the names—or are they? They're typing letters for bosses in offices, and I'm "fortunate" enough to be sitting in my apartment typing 3x5 cards and wishing I were printing photographs in my new darkroom.

The darkroom mocks me. "Okay, it says, "here I am, and what are you doing? You're still typing 3x5 cards. I'm waiting for you. Here I am, all set up and ready, and you're still killing yourself with that typing."

I turn on the radio, thinking maybe some music will cheer me up or at least make this dreadful work more bearable. I hear a singer singing a wistful song and I feel joyful and miserable. My tears are for myself: my lost dreams, the hopes of years past. I feel so much, I feel my own beauty and strength. I go back to typing so I can pay the rent.

At the close of the show in January 1976, I was back to square one financially, and facing another quandary about what lay ahead. Having invested four months in making, selecting, printing and framing 30 photographs, as well as planning, producing and promoting the show, I was broke and faced as always with paying the monthly bills. Tom had contributed many materials and immeasurable skills in matting and framing the photographs, and I had spent $1000 on the show and sold only one framed print. It was a familiar letdown after the big push to create the exhibit—another labor of love. My daughter's career was rapidly taking off, with accompanying recognition and financial rewards. I was happy for her, and depressed about my own situation. I did the best I could to keep my head above water, find work for pay. One project involved typing memoirs for Sis

Cunningham and Gordon Friesen, editors of *Broadside Magazine,* and helping them find a publisher for their autobiography. (*Red Dust and Broadside* was finally published in 1999 by University of Massachusetts Press.)

Five years earlier I had produced and promoted a concert to benefit *Broadside Magazine,* the 1960s-70s counterpart of the *People's Songs Bulletin* of the 40s. Held at Columbia University's McMillin Hall, it brought together performers and *Broadside* supporters Barbara Dane, Mabel Hillery, Janis Ian, Tulip Kupferberg, Ron Turner, Larry Estridge, Wes Huston and His Band, and Vicki Sue Robinson, billed as "jazz singer." I don't recall how much money we made, but I'm sure every penny helped Sis and Gordon to continue the feisty magazine that had published Bob Dylan's "Blowin' in the Wind," and provided a musical history of those years, a showcase in print for songwriters known and unknown.

Doing what I loved and going broke

In the letdown after the photography show, I saw a therapist twice a week and began to face the reality that I would have to find work that produced reliable income. After seven years building a professional career, here was another life transition, and it felt like a setback. I had to get a job again.

In a few months I was hired by the executive director of the International Tape Association (ITA) as editor of a bimonthly trade magazine in the up-and-coming home video and audio-videotape industry. Not that I knew much about this new technology. Larry Finley, my boss, gathered all the articles, photos, and ads, and my job was to handle the copyediting, layout, and production of a 40-page magazine for distribution to members of this prestigious organization—companies like SONY, JVC, Panasonic, Memorex, DuPont, Fuji Photo, 3M, Magnavox, RCA, TDK, and Video Corp. of America. For one issue, I researched and wrote an article titled, "Tape Shares Billing with Film at New York's Whitney Museum." It felt good to be using my research, language, and editorial skills in a professional capacity. In 1978, I flew to Tucson, Arizona for a three-day conference of ITA board members and executives. My suitcase went on to Los Angeles and I was without the clothes I had brought for the occasion. Larry Finley gave me money to buy a dress, and the suitcase arrived the next day.

To celebrate my 50th birthday in July 1978, I threw a big party at the studio and home of friend and sandal maker Barbara Shaum, whose backyard near Cooper Square would accommodate all the people we invited. It was a gala occasion, with old and new friends, along with Vicki and some of her friends. Right after that, Tom and I took a vacation trip to Colorado, where I met his family in Colorado Springs for the first time. Traveling through the Rocky Mountains was an awesome treat for this East Coast urban dweller.

As fate would have it, after I'd been at ITA a year, Larry Finley and I came to an impasse over his treatment of a black woman he hired as his "personal assistant." Larry could be arrogant in his dealings with employees, and I took him to task for the way he behaved toward this young woman who needed her job as much as I did. When we argued in his office, I quit—and was fired simultaneously! A few days later Larry called me saying he would tell the unemployment office I had been laid off so that I could collect unemployment compensation. I guess that was his decent side.

After months of unemployment and job search, a woman I had met in labor circles asked me to join the staff of a new Occupational Safety & Health (OSHA) department at the largest public sector union, District Council 37, AFSCME (American Federation of State, County and Municipal Employees). In addition to administrative duties, the job required editing and writing for the departmental newsletter I helped set up. Staff meetings were lively with good people, and I worked closely with union activists on various projects. Things were going well.

Crisis into opportunity?

In the late 70s, statewide Vacancy Decontrol undermined New York's Rent Control law, paving the way for "co-ops" and condo conversions. The landlord sold the seven-story building on 82nd Street to a corporation that planned to turn it into a co-op—meaning tenants would become shareholders—if the corporation could convince two-thirds of the tenants to vote for the plan. I worked to organize the tenants to resist the conversion, but after months of meetings to discuss the pros and cons, a majority of tenants voted to "buy in." I could hardly blame them because there were few options available in Manhattan. Vacancy decontrol meant that if you left your rent-controlled apartment for another, you faced "market rate" rents (three times higher). After meeting with a bank officer, it was clear that with my low income I could not get a mortgage. I had no choice but to move out of my home of 16 years where, even at my low rent, I had paid the owner $140,000 during my tenancy.

The idea of leaving New York was not new. I'd been thinking about it for some time. I had felt closed in by the city, its massive, tall buildings, the crowds, the noise, the extremes of freezing winters and hot, humid summers. I had photographed so much of the New York I loved, and I thought, "I've seen it, I've done it. I'm ready for a new vista. It's now or never." I wanted more space and nature. After all, I had come from a small village in a rural setting and I was getting older and needing a simpler life.

Tom and I had looked at some other possibilities—we thought Brattleboro, Vermont would be a lovely place to live, but how would we make a living? For awhile we considered the Baltimore area because Jac lived near there, and it was closer to Philadelphia and New York. We even looked at Colorado Springs when we visited Tom's parents in 1978. But that town is largely conservative and home to a huge military base, and we would feel like fish out of water. In 1979 we went to San Francisco on vacation. We stayed at a hotel in the city and visited friends who lived in Berkeley. We drove up the coast, saw some of the Bay Area, and fell in love with it.

Selling an apartment I didn't own

All hell broke loose after our California trip when the struggle began for the right to stay in my apartment. For seven long months it was up in the air—how would it be resolved, what would I do? The prospect of losing my apartment made me face the reality that if I were to make another move, it would have to be now. Though we had been living apart, I would not have considered California without Tom, and he didn't want to lose me, either.

There was one consolation. A lawyer who wanted to buy my apartment offered to pay me a sum of money in a quick turnaround—I would own the apartment for three days, after which it became legally his. His $24,000 payment made it possible to pay off some debts and have some money in the bank. The price he paid me was a fraction of what the apartment was soon worth in what was rapidly becoming an Upper West Side gentrified beyond recognition.

For months I had wrestled with the daunting prospect of leaving a good job, leaving my home, leaving the therapist who told me I wasn't ready to leave yet. It was hard to think of living so far from Amy, who at 75 had no desire to travel. Arden was only 120 miles from Manhattan and I'd been able to see her at least yearly, but California was another planet. Tom and I visited her before we left New York, and we all tried to be cheerful and positive. As she had done all her life, she took this news stoically, keeping her tears and sorrow to herself.

The toughest decision was putting 3000 miles between my daughter and me. Though I was not into 12-step programs then, I knew I was powerless over her drug addiction. At 25, with a career and friends and relatives in New York, Vicki's life was hers to live. It was an emotionally traumatic time. I was all too aware of her feelings about losing her mother after all she had been through with her father and her childhood. I arranged for her to move back into the apartment with a roommate and rent it from the new owner. We assured each other we would visit back and forth.

As it happened, visits were few and far between. Building a life in a new place takes time and a lot of work. I didn't get back East for three years, and not often after that.

Cultural Exchange Tour to the Soviet Union, 1971

```
HOTEL " SOVIETSKAYA "

LENINGRAD  L-16

LERMONTOVSKY  PROSPECT  43/1

TELEPHONE: 16-00 -32

STREET CARS No 1, 8, 9, 28, 29

TROLLEY-BUSES No 4, 8, 11, 13

BUS No 49

SUBWAY "BALTIYSKAYA" STATION

YOUR ROOM  1213
TELEPHONE  32-13
```

Above: Postcard to Vicki from Kiev

Left: Hotel data issued by Leningrad hotel

Below: Name tag worn on the tour to three cities, including Moscow. The tour was organized by the Citizen Exchange Corps as travel restrictions began to lift in the Khruschev regime.

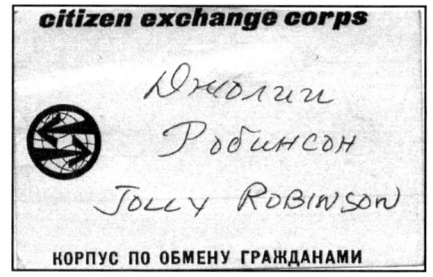

Staff members of Ms. Magazine include Alix, on her mother's lap, who goes to work three days a week. (Photo by Lois Smith)

The Unitarian Universalist Women's Federation May 1974 newsletter featured an article on women who work and raise children. Photo of *Ms.* Magazine staff members (Jolly is 2nd from left, back row).

CITY/COUNTRY IMPRESSIONS
Jolly Robinson • Jacquin Smolens
Photographs • Wood Sculpture

Opening Reception
Sunday December 7
One to Six p.m.
Through January 8

Hours: Tue-Fri, 4:30-8:30
Sat-Sun, 1-6

The Work of Art Gallery 87 Atlantic Avenue, Brooklyn Heights

Rural wood sculptures by Jac Smolens and urban photographs by Jolly Robinson occupied walls and space at the Work of Art Gallery, December 1975. Singers, musicians, and poets contributed to the festivities at holiday celebrations.

The Standard-Times, New Bedford, Mass.,
Wednesday, October 27, 1976

JOLLY ROBINSON

Folk singer due at SMU conference

Jolly Robinson, folk singer from New York, will appear at a women's conference, sponsored by the Labor Education Center, from 7:30 a.m. to noon Saturday at Southeastern Massachusetts University Group I Building.

A native of Arden, Delaware, Ms. Robinson has been singing folk songs since she was a child. Profoundly influenced by songwriter Woody Guthrie and others, she is actively involved in movements for jobs, housing, human rights, peace and freedom. She has given her "Labor Songs as History" program for colleges, unions and women's organizations.

The program also will include workshops on the Massachusetts Equal Rights Amendment. The amendment will appear as Question No. 1 on next Tuesday's ballot. Group leaders will be provided for discussion of the amendment and its implications.

A luncheon at 12:15 p.m. will follow the program. The fee for the conference, including lunch, is $5. For further information or reservations, contact Ms. Barbara S. Bruno, Division of Continuing Studies at SMU.

Left: Notice of my "Labor Songs as History" program at SMU. Above, from top: Central Park, late 60s; with Tom Schultz in Maryland; Amy walks with Tom on a rare visit to New York in the 70s.

A few of the Hoots and concerts Jolly appeared in or produced during the 1960s. She produced the "Perspectives" concert, in which Vicki Sue was billed as a jazz singer.

Singing at a clothing workers' protest picket line in front of Macy's (above) and a public employees' protest (below) against City Bank (now Citicorps) in the 1970s recession.

Left: Feminists demanding that *The New York Times* use "Ms." as a counterpart to "Mr." One sign says, "My Mrs. or Miss-ness Is Nobody's Business."

(Photos by Jolly Robinson)

Above and left: Two photos from my coverage of the International Women's Day March down 5th Avenue to Union Square, 1975.

Above: Welfare workers in the Bronx demonstrate against staff cuts.

Left: Postal workers demand decent pay for Vietnam veterans and other workers.

Above: Vicki Sue in the the early 70s in Manhattan.

Right: Singing at OG's Café.

Below: Taken the year before "Turn the Beat Around" was issued.

(Photos by Jolly Robinson)

CHAPTER FIVE
Starting Again in New Terrain

Arranging long distance to rent the Berkeley apartment wasn't easy. While I was still tied up with the job at District Council 37 and other commitments, Tom had gone to Berkeley for a month to arrange with the rental agent for us to move into the vacant apartment. On April 15, 1980, we said an emotional farewell to Vicki Sue in front of the building at 35 West 82nd Street, took a cab to the airport, and flew from New York to Oakland. I was about to see my new home for the first time.

We arrived in Berkeley with money from the sale of my apartment, but no job for either of us. The first order of business for me was to take driving lessons and get a license, and we bought a used Chevy sedan. I joined a support group to help ease the transition to a new place, and began looking for a job.

What I found was freelance proofreading work at California Continuing Education of the Bar (CEB), a legal publisher based in Berkeley tied to the State Bar and the University of California. CEB hired proofreaders as independent contractors on an hourly basis, usually three days a week. I made friends there and began to establish a social and professional network. For two years CEB provided a base from which to look for a full-time job. I joined other freelancers in an organizing effort by the union that represented campus employees, trying to get some basic benefits enjoyed by regular staff—Workers' Compensation and health care coverage. As it was, if we were laid off after working three days a week for years, we received no benefits.

Tom had been excited about the move after his month in Berkeley when he held the apartment and made arrangements. He had found a small carpentry job during his visit and was confident he'd have no problem finding work. But it wasn't long before the reality sank in that his familiar turf and friends and work connections were gone. As in New York, he relied mostly on local bars for networking. He made some contacts and got a few jobs. But as an artist he felt isolated and depressed. After sharing the apartment for a year and a half, I couldn't handle his drinking, moodiness, and erratic behavior. I told him how his drinking affected me and that I was trying to build a better life for myself. When I refused to back down, he found space in a friend's house in Oakland, where he lived and had studio space. After a period of not seeing each other, we resumed our friendship and continued to share a life as before.

For me, the break with job, friends, activities, and familiar networks on the East Coast created space to focus on things I had not had time for in New York, including a couple of writing classes and lots of reading of women writers. Tillie Olsen's *I Stand Here Ironing* and *Silences* and Adrienne Rich's *Of Woman Born* made profound impressions. Olsen spoke from her life experience of the difficulties working women encounter in finding time to write amid job and family demands. Rich was a more privileged woman struggling with issues of role expectations for women. Their different outlooks were shaped by class as well as gender. Olsen was my working class hero, and I liked Adrienne Rich as a feminist who sees class as a component of women's oppression along with gender and race. I wrote a personal reflection expressing the inner voices and conflicts I'd been dealing with for years.

The Tormenter

A nagging voice in my head keeps telling me I'll never write. Every time I sit down at the typewriter, the voice runs through its litany.

You've put off writing all these years; why should you start to write now? What makes you think you have something to say, and who will read it, anyhow?

I've heard all this before, but the Tormenter continues relentlessly.

Remember back when you were 18, you started singing for political causes? You were going to change the world? And how after barnstorming around the country you ended up broke and dependent on your father again? He sent you to secretarial school so you would settle down and make a living. Writing? What a nerve to think you can write!

Ignoring my pleas to stop, the Tormenter gets louder and more sarcastic.

Sure, you moved back to New York when you were 35 to try for a singing career. You actually thought you'd get paid for singing. But you forgot that you were a mother first, a secretary second, and singing was a luxury you couldn't afford.

I've had just about enough, but the taunting escalates.

Then, when you were 41 you thought you'd go to college. You even got funded to do a research project that involved writing, but when it was over you were out of work again. You didn't get a degree because your daughter was a teenager and you still had to work full-time. You couldn't hack it.

I argue with the Tormenter. "But I wanted to do photography then. You don't need a degree for that." Now the Tormenter is merciless.

HA! Look what happened when you tried to do photography at 45. You had to type and do clerical work for other people so you could pay the rent. Without part-time jobs, unemployment, and help from Tom you'd never have done it.

"Yes, but I did it. I got my photographs published and even produced exhibits of my own work." Right on cue, the Tormenter sticks the knife in and twists it.

So where did that get you? After that show you were more in debt than ever. You were so depressed you got into therapy, dyed your hair, and got a job again.

I can't take this abuse any longer. "Go to hell! I won't listen to you. Get lost!"

In the ominous silence, I am alone. I close my eyes and try to focus. Barely audible, through much static, a small voice is trying to get through, urging me to listen . . .

They all want a piece of me

It's not easy to escape the fragmentation of a lifetime of survival necessities and gender roles. After all the years of working at office jobs, being breadwinner, wife, mother, and singer/political activist, I feel drained, exhausted. I have given so much away it sometimes seems there is nothing left for me. In a poem I wrote in 1978:

> *They all want a piece of me—*
> *Vicki, and Tom, and*
> *yesterday it was my photography teacher*
> *and my therapist*
> *and my women's group*
> *and the landlord*
> *and the bank*
> *and the bill collectors*
> *and the department stores*
> *and the state*
> *and the feds*

and my neighbors
and my friends
and my mother
and causes that want money
and the grocery, cleaner, laundry, post office,
doctor, dentist, hospital, clinic
and my bosses, god knows,
and co-workers
and neighbors
and my apartment
and my clothes
yes, even my photography equipment.
They all want a piece of the action
and the action
is me.

Can I ever gather my thoughts, hold on to them, develop them fully, place a value on them? Can I permit myself time for reflection, imagination, focusing, creative thinking?

When I write, the words often come out in short, clipped phrases, as if I must hurry and spit them out fast before the door opens and Tom walks in, or the phone rings, or I have to get to the store before it closes, or . . . How can I believe that I'll have an hour to develop a whole sentence or follow an idea to where it takes me? Can I give myself the space and time, the support that has rarely come from others? How shall I place myself and my own work, my writing, in the center? And then what urgent new reality will come along to disrupt my plans for writing?

Tillie Olsen, author of *Tell Me a Riddle* and *Silences*, saw her first novel published when she was 50. She speaks for me when she describes women writers' conditioning by sex role and class imperatives.

"The habits of a lifetime when everything else had to come before writing are not easily broken. Even when circumstances now often make it possible for writing to be first; habits of years—response to others, distractibility, responsibility for daily matters—stay with you, mark you, become you. The cost of "discontinuity" . . . is such a weight of things unsaid, an accumulation of material so great, that everything starts up something else in me; what should take weeks takes me sometimes months to write; what should take months, takes years."

—Tillie Olsen, *Silences* (New York: Dell Publishing Co., 1978)

Even when I do manage to clear a space for writing, the years of being distracted, interrupted, preempted, responsible to and for others often push my own priorities into a dim attic closet. There they lurk in tangled, shadowy forms, threatening either to rush out in an uncontrollable flood, or to stay shut away safely in the attic. Vague, elusive images vie with each other for attention. "Don't go for the big event," says a writing teacher. Lots of luck. They're all big. Overwhelming. Inseparable.

Small voice, growing

Everything in my life has led me to this place, this poetry, this confrontation with self. Through all the dead-end office jobs, the rush hour subways, the endless rounds of housework, the uncharted course of single motherhood in the 50s and 60s, the small voice inside has been getting more insistent, prodding me to clear away the debris, carve out a space, claim it for myself.

Come out of the closet, the voice tells me. You are the source—your life, your experience. You are the authority. I'm listening.

I had been through menopause and was noticing the changes in my body. Having learned from my grandmother's healthy lifestyle, I gravitated toward the alternative and holistic health practices that abound in the Bay Area—chiropractic, body movement classes, acupuncture, massage, and nutrition counseling, among others. An MD who was open to alternative medicine headed the Berkeley Holistic Health Center, and I sought out practitioners whom I continued to see over the years. Though it may not have been wholly conscious at the time, I'm sure that moving toward a healthier lifestyle was both a motivation for and a benefit of coming to the Bay Area. I found support groups or classes for everything from aging and women's issues to writing, computer skills, and career development. I wanted to get support and education from many sources.

Vicki's first visit

Vicki came for Christmas the first year we were here. So did my long-lost first cousin Phyllis and her husband Frank Thomas, who lived in Los Angeles. It started out as a happy reunion, with Christmas Eve together and Vicki busily helping prepare Christmas dinner in the new apartment. The next day she went to visit an old friend in San Francisco and failed to show up for the party I gave in her honor. It turned out she had cashed in her return trip plane ticket to buy drugs. When she came back full of remorse, she asked if she could leave her things with me while she went to LA to get work. After agonizing about it over a sleepless night, I told her what I was willing to do was to pay her air fare to return to New York and her life. It was another wrenching decision, but I knew it would be best for both of us. We said a tearful goodbye at the airport, one of so many farewells before and afterwards. Hello and goodbye, an old story that lives in my poems and in my heart, as in this poem, written years earlier.

Endings and beginnings

Endings and beginnings
saying goodbye and hello
something finished something begun
one step forward
how many steps back
one step sideways
steps avoided
goodbye
hello.

I take your leave
wave at you across the platform
not knowing when we'll meet again
if ever.

I didn't know it would end
so abruptly
and
I wanted to make a space
between
today and
what tomorrow will bring
but
I got carried away
by what today demanded
and what tomorrow could wait for.
The known
the unknown
is it forward or backward or sideways
or overlapping
one thing tried

three things missed
avoided
postponed.

It's true.
There is no tomorrow.

In 1983 I made two big decisions. I entered Al-Anon at the urging of a friend who knew that two people in my life had troubling addictions—my daughter and Tom. I was painfully aware that significant people in my life had been addicts and/or alcoholics, and that I had done my share of drinking. While I had resisted 12-step programs because of the religious emphasis, in Berkeley many others felt as I did, and some of the language in the 12-step rituals had been revised to make them less "God-oriented," allowing for individual interpretation of "higher power." I attended many meetings and learned a lot about codependency: first and foremost, that I cannot change anyone but myself, and that's a tough enough job. It's the only leaderless group I've experienced that works well over time, because of its established structure and format at every meeting.

The second big decision was to reclaim my given name, Marianne, after I'd lived 54 years as Jolly. Starting anew in a place removed from the first half of my life meant that I constantly had to explain my first name. "Is that your real name?" was the most frequent question. Then there was "Oh, like Jolly Green Giant!" Mail came addressed to Mr. Jolly Robinson. It was the most personal, yet public, decision I had ever made, and the effects were both immediate and long-lasting. Changing the name on everything, from my Social Security card to every piece of identification, meant paperwork and red tape. Hardest was announcing the change to relatives and long-time friends, and trying to explain when people asked, "What made you decide to do that?" I finally arrived at the simple answer: "I got tired of being an adjective." Though I was never sorry I had made the change, I faced the fall-out from it for years.

Somewhere in the 70s, my brother Jac and his wife Jean had separated, and their four children remained with him in Maryland. As each left home in their teens, Coby, Teri, and Mundi ended up in California, while Rai landed in Michigan. At nearly 50, Jac had married Lisa, a younger woman with whom he had a son, Kaili. Jac, Lisa, and baby Kaili visited me in Berkeley in 1982 on a trip to the West Coast. Eight years later, they adopted a Paraguayan child whose name was Andrian. Given our complicated lives, Jac and I saw each other seldom in the years after I left the East Coast. I did manage to get back East several times, but Jac's family and his work as a wood sculptor kept him close to home.

For three months in 1981, I was hired by the Labor Occupational Health Program (LOHP) at UC Berkeley to edit and produce *A Health and Safety Handbook for Local Unions.* In addition to editing the entire book, I wrote the last chapter, "Building Support," which was closely related to my experience working with unions. When the book was finished, I returned to proofreading at CEB for awhile. Then, in the absence of editing work, I answered an ad for office support for Live Oak Institute, a nonprofit dedicated to "regenerative community in nursing homes." I joined a small group of professionals in the research and development phase of a model program for nursing homes. Besides office administration, I helped edit and produce a brochure to promote the Live Oak model to the nursing home industry. After nearly two years, I was laid off when Live Oak ran out of funding. It was déjà vu as I revisited the unemployment line for six months and worked briefly for an entrepreneur on a marketing project before quitting in frustration over his mixed messages about pay and working conditions.

The Live Oak directors, Barry and Debby Barkan, continued their dedicated work and remained friends over the years. I worked with them on several publication projects, including a staff training manual and a book of poems by residents of a nursing home they bought and managed in order to implement their Elders Program.

In 1983, Tom stopped drinking. He went to AA meetings for nearly three years with a friend in the program. Gradually he began drinking again, except for one short period in the 90s. But that ended with a trip to Germany to exhibit his paintings. He said he couldn't resist the German beer.

Amy's California sojourn

For her 80th birthday in September 1984, Amy made the long voyage to visit me. She decided it was now or never and, sticking to her refusal to fly, traveled by train all the way across the country, a three-day trip. When we met her at the Oakland station, she was exhausted, looking as pale and thin as a ghost. For the first three days she didn't leave my apartment but sat at the dining room table or in the back yard, recuperating from the arduous journey. She had come to visit her daughter, and to fulfill her dream of seeing California before she died. The three things she had always wanted to see were the Pacific Ocean, the Golden Gate Bridge, and the San Francisco cable cars. It was an eye-opening experience for me, too, having never seen my mother so far from her home and environment.

Amy enjoyed walking around my neighborhood in Berkeley, seeing the trees and flowers and yards around people's houses, and getting into conversations about plants and gardens. She was happy to sit a spell when we came to a bench in front of someone's house. I was keenly aware of how much older she seemed than when I'd seen her in Arden just a year before. When we took her in the car to the Berkeley Hills to show her the view overlooking the bay, she was terrified by the height and the winding road at the top of the steep cliff. In San Francisco, when we drove down Lombard Street with its U turns at 5 miles per hour, she hid her eyes, saying she couldn't look. "Why would anyone want to live here?" she asked.

I had never realized how provincial and fearful my mother was—or had become in her old age. She did enjoy the beach at the Pacific Ocean, but was disappointed that the Golden Gate Bridge looked pink—not gold at all, or even red! She did not want to drive across the bridge, having heard stories of how it sways in high winds. And she was dismayed to find the cable cars open on all sides. She clung to her bench seat and dealt with her fears by chatting with the people around her and avoiding the roller coaster views.

When we took her to the train and said goodbye after two weeks, it was another sad parting, and I know she feared that she might never see me again. As it turned out, I was able to visit her in Arden several times before she died at 89.

A good job—finally

That October, just after Amy's visit, I was hired by the State Bar of California to design, produce and edit a bimonthly, statewide newsletter to go to every member of the Bar and its staff. It also went to the California Judicial Council, and to State legislators who voted yearly on setting the mandatory fees paid by lawyers. The headquarters were in a large building in San Francisco near Civic Center. I was hired on a three-quarter time basis with good pay and benefits and was given a small office of my own. It was a welcome opportunity, the best and most challenging job I ever had for an employer. State Bar staff, including attorneys, were members of Service Employees International Union (SEIU) Local 250, a strong local union that Bar employees had chosen because of its democratic policies and leadership.

I produced the newsletter, *Grapevine,* in the prevailing mode—electric typewriter, paper, paste-up and photo prints—and took it to a commercial printer for reproduction and printing. I conducted interviews by phone, or contacted State Bar personnel to request articles and news briefs which I edited for the newsletter. In those pre-electronic days, material had to be faxed or mailed for editing and approval, and before the newsletter went to press, all its content had to be approved by the State Bar's director. I worked closely with the woman who had hired me, who was familiar with the turf and served as liaison in official matters. We would go over plans for each issue based on developments within the Bar, and then I was on my own. For me, contacting, interviewing, and working with the people and programs and departments that contributed to each issue was thoroughly enjoyable, and varied widely for each issue.

At that time, the State Bar was having internal struggles over the "policing" of lawyers as well as the perennial controversy about how lawyers' membership fees were to be spent. During my tenure, the union called a strike—and for the first time anywhere, staff lawyers were out on the picket line, along with department heads, clerical staff, and mailroom workers. For more than a year after the strike, I worked hard to defend my job or redefine it according to changing priorities, but when a reorganization at the top took place in early 1988, I was laid off with several others. The newsletter I had created three years before was discontinued—the baby thrown out with the bath water. I was out of a job again at nearly 60. I collected the accrued benefits I had earned in the job I'd hoped to retire from, and applied for Unemployment Compensation. For some years I attempted to get freelance work from people on Bar staff, but nothing ever came of it.

Social and spiritual community

One Sunday morning in 1987, feeling depressed and at loose ends, I walked into the Unitarian Universalist Fellowship just three blocks from home. My job was insecure, I felt alienated from Tom, who was drinking again, and my daughter was 3000 miles away. I'd been to musical events at Fellowship Hall and had wondered what happened on Sundays at this small church in my neighborhood. My grandfather had gone to meetings at a Unitarian church in Delaware, but I knew next to nothing about Unitarianism or what a church service was like.

They say there's a time and a place for everything, and this was my time, my place. My wandering and questioning and seeking had brought me to this small church in this neighborhood in this city, far from my roots and my past connections—or so I thought. As it turned out, I found myself in the midst of a lively congregation of souls where differences were respected and welcomed. I didn't have to believe in God or any religious dogma.

The service that morning was by the minister, Paul Sawyer, and while I don't recall the topic, I do remember how warmly I was greeted by the minister and members of the congregation, and how much at home I felt in that hall among those people. A few months later, I joined the Berkeley Fellowship of Unitarian Universalists and became active in congregational life. Among many other activities, I redesigned the monthly newsletter, *The Communicator,* and began editing and producing it in 1993.

Internal Landscape

These days
instead of bars
      booze
            pavements
      subways
            high-rise apartments
      office jobs
                 brokenhearted love affairs
      parenting
            politics
                 and photography…
my landscape is
      cafés
            back yard
                 tawny hills
      winding roads
            cars
                 freeways
      computers
            new friends
                 new discoveries
and a spiritual community.

The world outside has changed, while
in my internal landscape, familiar road signs—

transience
      alienation
                fragmentation

     survival struggles
              search for connection
                        living on the edge—
give way to new vistas.

The road looks different now.
Boulders still clutter the landscape
     but instead of insurmountable obstacles
        they look more like the rocks they always were.

In the long, twisting tunnel of my life
I have fought and
     kicked and
     SHOUTED!
     trying to find the light.

These days
     on my spiritual journey,
I follow my own beacon in the night.

Turning her life around

    Vicki had moved out of the 82nd Street apartment and was living with friends in Connecticut and pursuing her career as a singer. We had kept in frequent touch, and she usually came for Christmas with us in Berkeley. In 1985 she entered AA and ended her drinking and drugging once and for all. When she visited in 1986, she sang at an outdoor anti-apartheid concert with Danny Kalb of the Blues Project, went jogging at the waterfront and to the local gym for fitness work-outs. Then she wrote that she was going with "Billy," and in early 1988 she brought Bill Good to meet us and announced that they were planning to be married the following year. On that visit, Vicki sang some of our familiar folk song duets with me in a Sunday service at the Fellowship. (Tom made an audiotape, the only recording I have of our mother/daughter duo.) It was a wonderful visit in all ways, with my daughter looking radiantly happy and in love, and singing with her Mom as in earlier times!

    I often said her hit song, "Turn the Beat Around," should be renamed "Turn Your Life Around." Vicki had shown her inner strength by putting 15 years of addiction behind her, had followed her true calling in music and performance, and was about to marry the loving partner who would share the rest of her life.

Setting up shop

After being laid off by the State Bar, I began yet another job search. When nothing came of it and unemployment compensation ran out, I decided to invest in a Macintosh computer and set up shop at home. Tom built a fine L-shaped counter, file drawers, shelves, and a table in the small second bedroom in my apartment. I would become a consultant specializing in client publications and special projects. Not only would I have to find the clients, but I would have to learn enough about the computer and the new desktop publishing software to produce professional results in a competitive market. I decided to call my business Publishing Solutions, which appeared on my stationery and letterhead, and registered with the county as a small business. For the first seven or eight years business was conducted entirely without the benefit of the Internet or email, involving computer technology, hard copy, fax or postal transmission (or delivery by car to the client or printer) and offset printing.

I signed up for an intensive workshop with women trying to get their businesses going, and took a basic Macintosh computer class and some private graphics training. The best outcome of the business group was meeting a woman who came to my office and gave me instruction in the new PageMaker design and layout software while I designed a newsletter for a prospective client. It was hands-on training and application on a real project, always the way I learned best. I developed a network of business contacts and a mailing list, produced a promotional brochure, and acquired a couple of client projects within a year. In 1988-89 I had the advantage of skills that were new in the world of business and nonprofits, but this would change rapidly as the technology became widespread and much of what I did as an independent contractor was being done by in-house employees.

Part of a letter I sent to Amy on my new business letterhead read:

It is a mystery, isn't it—the twists and turns in the road that lead us far from where we started? Why doesn't the mouse in the maze stay where it was to begin with? Why does it always seek to find where the road leads and follow it around each corner? (Would it stay home if there were no food at the end of the maze?) I suppose there are some mice that are too timid to stray, or who choose not to see what's around the next corner. But I was never one of those.

My restless nature has led me to continue striving, trying new things, taking risks, pushing the limits—they say this is a characteristic of creative people. My native curiosity has led me along the path my grandparents on both sides traveled—a philosophical, social, political quest, including a commitment to work with others for change. In recent years, as with many folks growing older, my spiritual quest has emerged and become prominent. [Referring to joining the UU Fellowship.]

As much as I enjoyed the challenge and satisfaction of taking on new projects, self-employment was a roller coaster ride, much as it had been in New York in the 70s—only my focus then was photography and teaching; now it involved writing, editing, graphic design and publication skills. Some projects involved designing and producing brochures or marketing materials. There were training manuals, catalogs, annual reports, and booklets that involved client meetings and intensive research. Specialized terminology presented a constant challenge to learn and keep up to speed. I put together books, anthologies, and biographies for individuals, and brochures for local political campaigns. Newsletters could involve any combination of interviewing, writing, editing, formatting, design and layout, handling photos and pre-press production, and coordinating with an offset printer. There was much time-consuming back-and-forth with clients in securing the material, making revisions, and getting approvals. I became expert at estimating, negotiating, and writing contracts.

Satisfactions and setbacks

Over the course of 17 years, I produced publications for clients that ranged from a newsletter for six years to a one-time training handbook or annual report that took three to six months to complete. Producing a brochure could take several months, while interviewing people for a series of profiles could be completed in weeks. After the training manual I'd done for the Labor Occupational Health Program at UC Berkeley, they hired me for several complex publications that stretched over a period of years. One project was terminated when staff couldn't do their part on schedule and my time was being extended well beyond the contract. I secured several public sector projects for Alameda County, including two newsletters and several brochures. When the projects fell through for lack of funding or were taken over by staff, it was back to the drawing board to seek other clients and projects.

Several start-to-finish projects gave me great satisfaction and a lot of room to use my creative skills and experience. One was designing, writing, and producing a 24-page booklet describing community organizations for East Bay Funders, a consortium of grant-making institutions in East Oakland and Richmond. Over several months, along with the director and a photographer, I visited the organizations and interviewed individuals who lived and worked in those neighborhoods. We walked through playgrounds and visited community centers, schools, and the homes of neighbors. The on-site interviews offered priceless education and insights into what I was expected to write about, and it resulted in one of the best publications I ever produced. Tom designed a beautiful logo for the cover, and I gave it its title, "Putting the Pieces Together—Community Collaboratives at Work." As in Margaret Mead's projects and my travels with the Caravans, it was a truly collaborative project that couldn't have happened without the participation of many individuals at every step.

East Oakland

Rosa Domingo and her children
Rosa with the indomitable spirit
smile to light up the world
Maria and Helena, 11 going on adult
beautiful, tender young faces
having seen so much in their child years
fearful of stepping on hypodermic needles
in the sand of the playground

> Emilio Navarro the outspoken priest from El Salvador
> his ministry the people
> in the apartment building where he lives
> getting smoke alarms and hall lights
> jobs for new immigrants from Mexico or El Salvador
> sharing a small room, kitchen and bath
> with a night-shift worker who sleeps during the day
> covered in a shroud-like sheet
> Emilio, teaching children from a book he wrote
> in the language of his country
> bringing hope into people's lives

Starting Again In New Terrain

Joe Wilson, 83, who stayed when other white folks fled
his wife and friends long gone
who gives away vegetables from his garden
especially to the poorer people
says "I have more than I can use"
stalwart member of the 33rd Avenue Block Association
Joe has seen many changes
has learned to love his neighbors

> Robert Bailey, cheerful, weathered face
> left arm missing
> came from St. Louis long ago with few skills
> played briefly with the San Francisco Black baseball team
> retired from his job with the Army after 29.7 years
> for 35 years a role model for neighborhood youth
> his organic garden has roses, tomatoes, sugar cane, lemon grass
> he proudly shows us his home-canned pickled mushrooms and okra
> seasoned salt and salami herb bread
> "There used to be 137 children living on this street and I knew them all,"
> says Robert.

James McDonald, unofficial mayor of Sobrante Park
greeting everyone by first name
settling disputes between storekeepers
and residents in the neighborhood
where he grew up
giving back
what he got from the elders who stood by him
through the drug years
the jail years
now James is a model for young kids
working at his first real job
in the office of the community organization
getting his high school diploma at 37

Another satisfying project was working with the staff of Homeward Bound of Marin to create its Spring 1998 Community Report on the transition from homelessness. In five housing and support centers in lower Marin County, I interviewed residents with diverse backgrounds about the circumstances and experiences that had led them to the resources they needed to get back on their feet. With photographs of each person interviewed, the stories in the words of real people enlivened the oversized, 8-page publication for donors and supporters of Homeward Bound.

Steady clients were few and far between, income was never the same from one month or year to the next, and cash flow resembled the Dow-Jones graph. I learned that doing multi-task projects from start to finish meant being paid far below the going rate for each applied skill. Whereas proofreading a manuscript involved one skill charged hourly or by the page, producing a newsletter encompassed multiple transactions, skills and hours folded into a project fee. Self-employed professionals in this field, I discovered, were routinely under-compensated for the sum total of their time, skills, and experience. As with most of the work I had enjoyed and found meaningful, it was underpaid or short-term, or both.

No guarantees

After I'd been in my apartment for five years, it did not come as a big surprise that Rent Control was under attack by the State of California. When the property interests could not get rid of Rent Control (officially Rent Stabilization) in the few cities where it existed, they succeeded in weakening Rent Control ordinances statewide by instituting "vacancy decontrol." This meant that when a rent-controlled apartment became vacant, the landlord could raise the rent as high as the market would allow, so that a new tenant could be charged two or three times the rate for the same unit. I wholeheartedly joined the fierce campaign for effective Rent Control and in the process earned a few dollars for pro-tenant brochures and flyers I created. Tenants and other Berkeley voters succeeded in strengthening the Rent Stabilization Board so that a majority of progressives made up the Board. The property owners' organizations continued their fight against Rent Control, but they got the message that they had not won the hearts and minds of most Berkeley voters.

The best of times

May 10, 1989 was the date set for Vicki's wedding in Connecticut. (Coincidentally, May 10 was the date Tom and I had met!) She and Bill paid our air fare and put us up at a charming suburban hotel in Weston. Vicki had spent many months enthusiastically planning every detail of this major event in her life. She took me to elegant shops in Westport to find dresses and shoes and bags for the pre-wedding dinner and the big wedding ceremony that was held on the grounds of a beautiful park with a wedding chapel. Tom rented a tuxedo for the wedding, the first and only time he ever wore one! I felt like a fish out of water during all these preparations, felt the contrast between my daughter's life and my own. But I understood her strong need for ceremony and ritual, coming from a non-traditional background where family affairs were casual and unceremonious. She was so proud to have her mother with her on this milestone occasion that symbolized the love and happiness she had found in her personal life that not even her successful career could match.

As mother of the bride, I escorted Vicki Sue, looking like a radiant goddess in her white dress and sparkling tiara, along the path from the main hall to the Grecian style outdoor chapel. Relatives and guests sat in rows of chairs on the lawn while the ceremony was performed by the minister Vicki and Bill had chosen. The sky was darkening, and just as the bride and groom made it to the hall, with everyone following behind them, the rain clouds burst and we were drenched from head to foot. Inside, we mingled with relatives and guests, enveloped by the magic glow of the just-married couple and the wedding spirit. Outside, under a big canopy as the rain let up, Bill and Vicki cut the wedding cake and the band played for dancing. It had to have been the happiest moment of Vicki Sue's life. I was so overcome by tumultuous emotions that I hardly knew whether I was coming or going. Bill and Vicki were renting a house not far away, and would soon move into their own home in Wilton, near the wedding site. It came to symbolize the best and worst times for my daughter—and my memories of Connecticut.

Natural disasters

Back in California, my self-employment was in its second year, with alternating work and seeking work, and growing involvement in the life of the UU Fellowship. That year the big earthquake shook Northern California and people's complacency. I was not directly affected, but it served as the wake-up call that living in desirable California was not without its risks. Two years later, the big firestorm swept through the East Bay Hills, demolishing everything in its path and sending an even stronger warning to residents that, despite the privilege of living in the hills, no one is exempt from nature's ravages.

Reverie

I'm hanging clothes on the line
In my back yard
After the big firestorm
As I did the night of the earthquake
Just two years ago.

This corner of the back yard
Shared by day with birds and squirrels and cats
At night with raccoons, possums and skunks
Speaks to me of Gaia
The power of Mother Earth
And the universe we're part of.

In the act of hanging clothes to dry
As my mother and grandmother did
Under the bright blue sky
Breeze scented with fall leaves
Ground firm underfoot

A revelation overtakes me
Here, in the corner of my back yard
As I hang clothes to dry in the sweet air.
A fusion with nature
With people and other beings
Who've lost their homes
Or their lives
From fires
From earthquakes
From poverty
From starvation
And other disasters of systems
Natural and unnatural.
Contemplating the human condition

Sorrow, loss and grief mingle with
Hope and grateful breath
As I fasten a sheet with clothespins
In this sacred corner
Of my back yard.

I had continued writing poetry in the "new world," and one Sunday in 1990, after a service at the Fellowship, I read a poem aloud during the dialog period. A man approached me afterwards and invited me to read at a poetry series at the North Berkeley Senior Center. So began the new experience of reading my poems at open mikes and as a featured poet in the East Bay and San Francisco.

Post-Christmas blues

A year and a half after the wedding, Vicki invited us to come for Christmas in the house they had bought in Wilton. Again, she paid our fare and planned a holiday party, and they were excited about the new recording studio Bill had set up in the basement of their home. Despite an abscessed tooth that was troublesome, I decided to go, take painkillers, and get to the dentist when I came back. To make a long story short, the visit was difficult for me and a big disappointment for Vicki, who had held great expectations for having her mother come for Christmas in her first real home. In January I mailed my usual year-end message to relatives and friends, mentioning the Christmas visit with other highlights of my year. There was no word from Vicki for nearly two months. Then a letter came saying that she was angry that I had barely mentioned our Christmas together; I had been selfish; she needed to get on with her life and would not be in touch for awhile. I was devastated and felt like I had lost my daughter forever. I heaped blame on myself and hardly slept at all. Without contact with Vicki, the days were endless. Paul Sawyer, the minister at the Fellowship, found me crying on my way home from church one Sunday and listened as I poured out my grief and sorrow. Finally, after weeks, I found words to write Vicki a letter of amends. Two weeks later a package arrived with a framed photo of the two of us looking into each other's eyes as we dressed for her wedding. Her note said she had been relieved to get my letter—"I needed to hear that, Mom, all of it."

On the music front in California from 1980, I did more arranging and producing of events than performing as a singer. I booked composer Earl Robinson, who wrote "The House I Live In" and many famous songs, for an annual gathering of the Meiklejohn Civil Liberties Institute in Berkeley. With the help of Eliot Kenin and others, I produced "Songs for Organizing," a workshop for singer/activists held on the UC Berkeley campus, featuring Charlie King with Martha Leader and local singer/songwriters. Eleanor Walden, a friend from Arden days, had co-founded the Freedom Song Network, and I took part in its activities at political demonstrations.

Though I sang and led songs at the Fellowship, by the late 90s, singing gave way to poetry as my primary creative expression, and I enjoyed reading at many local venues.

Photography had taken a back seat in New York by the late 1970s. After my cameras were stolen, I had sold the darkroom equipment and focused on other work. In California, where I made only small color prints, I could afford neither the time nor the cost of printing, preparing, and exhibiting them. In 1993 I was inspired to research, develop, and teach a photography class at a Berkeley Adult School. Called "Your World, Your Vision," its purpose was to encourage students to photograph what interested them in their everyday environment and share the results with the class. It was a stimulating experience with a small group, but classes were on weekday evenings, and field trips had to be arranged on weekends. The class dwindled to four or five students and, though I had received certification to teach again, the pay was minimal, and I declined in favor of my editing and publishing business.

Tom had been painting more in California than he had ever done back East. His use of bold color and the introduction of a hard-edge element had taken him in new directions with his abstractions. He had produced a sizable body of work and had shown at local galleries. In 1995 he was invited by a dealer to exhibit his work at Amerika Haus in Stuttgart, Germany. While in Germany, he found a gallery in Köln that wanted to handle his paintings. He continued to show and sell there until the gallery pulled some shady deals, after which he was unable to retrieve five of his large paintings. He exhibited regularly at the Louvre, a San Francisco gallery, until it went out of business. He learned firsthand the perils of art as a commodity in a market system where the artist and the gallery need each other, but the gallery owners set the terms.

One community, many activities

From 1993 on, editing and producing the Fellowship newsletter, *The Communicator*, kept me in touch with the ongoing life of the congregation. In early 1994, the minister left after a polarizing controversy, and the congregation became lay-led. To promote healing and reconciliation, I initiated and participated in a reevaluation process that involved the congregation and helped us move on. Over a four-month period, with a UU facilitator, many of us met on weekends to sort out and discuss important aspects of Fellowship life. We called it the "Voyage of Discovery" as we re-visioned ourselves as a lay-led congregation.

I produced and publicized Fellowship concerts, forums and events, and participated in Sunday programs, especially those marking International

Women's Day, May Day, the Anniversary of Hiroshima, and Labor Day, and contributed as speaker, singer, poet, or coordinator. During her visit at Christmas 1995, Vicki Sue joined me once again in singing, another unforgettable experience. I helped to organize a forum series that featured media critic Ben Bagdikian and others, and produced a sold-out concert with the Vukani Mawethu Choir and its songs of South African struggles. For three and a half years, I produced and hosted a monthly open mike series with featured artists and a dedicated crew who pitched in to set up the hall, handle the sound system, take donations at the door, and serve refreshments. It was a successful cultural series that brought performers and audience from the wider community to share poetry, music, and spoken word in an informal atmosphere around candlelit tables. There was a small budget to cover expenses, and we took in enough to contribute to the Fellowship coffers. For me, this undertaking was truly a labor of love, bringing people together to share and promote their creative talents.

Over the years at the Fellowship, I saw many changes in demographics, leadership, budget and program priorities, and an ongoing struggle to balance spiritual and political concerns. Individuals came with different needs, ideas, and hopes—and some left in frustration and disillusionment. Others who had been pillars of the congregation died or moved away. And some remained through thick and thin.

This small, ever-changing congregation of people from different backgrounds and lives became a center for many of my interests and energies. I experienced the Fellowship as a community in which I had a history; where differences and similarities with others could be celebrated and shared. I wrote and spoke about Arden as my first community and how that matrix, that early experience of community of freethinkers, led me over a long and winding road to the Berkeley Fellowship of Unitarian Universalists.

SONGS FOR ORGANIZING
A WORKSHOP FOR ACTIVISTS WITH

CHARLIE KING **MARTHA LEADER**

SATURDAY, FEBRUARY 11, 2-5 PM
U. C. BERKELEY

Bancroft
Student Union
Top Floor
Telegraph

Admission $5.00
$3.00 Unemployed
& Disabled

Please Post

LABOR DONATED

SONGS FOR ORGANIZING

A WORKSHOP WITH
CHARLIE KING & MARTHA LEADER

Saturday, Feb. 11, 2-5 pm
U.C. Student Union, Tilden Room
Berkeley

ADMIT ONE
$5.00 ADMISSION

Publicity, ticket, and program for "Songs for Organizing," a labor of love (and love of labor) produced in 1984. The 3-hour workshop brought together singers and songwriters from the Bay Area to show how activists use songs and singing in labor and political organizing.

```
SONGS FOR ORGANIZING

2:00    DOORS OPEN
        Table at door for tickets, money, sign-up sheet,
        songsheets, etc.
2:15    Introduction to Workshop/Marianne
2:20    CHARLIE & MARTHA
3:00    BAYAREA SONGWRITERS
        Jon Fromer              Jose Luis Oroszco
        Linda Hirschhorn        Paul McKenna
        Russ Scheidler          Joan Moore
        Ed Dick                 Faith Petric
        Rafael Manriquez        Sachiko
        Fundi                   Eliot Kenin
        Irving Fromer with      Bruce Thomas
          Eleanor Walden,
          Marianne Robinson
4:20    DISCUSSION LED BY CHARLIE
5:00    WRAP-UP/Marianne
        Eleanor on Freedom Song Network
        Announce June Political Song Gathering
        Distribute Resource Sheets

        CLOSING SONG/Charlie & Martha with cast of thousands
```

Poster by Campaign Against Apartheid for a rally in Berkeley's Civic Center Plaza, 1986. Danny Kalb of the former Blues Project accompanied Vicki Sue on guitar.

Vicki Sue performing onstage with Danny Kalb at the anti-apartheid rally in Berkeley.

Wedding Pictures, May 10, 1989

Vicki and her Mom prepare in the dressing room.

Mom escorts her daughter down the path toward the outdoor chapel.

The newly married couple cut the wedding cake.

Mom and Tom dance after the ceremony.

Mother and daughter on a day trip along the California coast.

Vicki visits Tom at his studio in the 90s.

An eagerly awaited Christmas visit in Berkeley, 1995.

Tom with Jack Micheline, poet and painter, at a show of Tom's paintings at the Berkeley Art Center, 1985.

PHOTOGRAPHY WORKSHOP
"Your World, Your Vision"

Do you just "point and shoot"?

Learn to define your unique way of seeing and get it across to others through the medium of photography.

You don't need sophisticated equipment or years of training. Using any 35mm camera, you can sharpen your personal vision and learn to make good photographs.

By practicing on assignments between classes, field trips with the class, looking at lots of photographs, and critiquing the work in class, you will improve your skills, your confidence and your "camera eye." The instructor and guest photographers will also show and talk about their work.

No darkroom facilities are provided. Students will be responsible for their own film and processing. A list of local photography outlets and resources will be supplied.

➤ *Where:* Berkeley Adult School
1222 University Avenue
Berkeley CA 94702-1709
510-644-6130

➤ *When:* Wednesdays, 7-9 PM
September 29 thru December 15

➤ *Instructor:* Marianne Robinson

➤ *Cost:* $56

➤ *Registration:* Monday-Friday 8 AM-3:45 PM
Tuesday, Sept. 21 only: 6-8 PM
At the Berkeley Adult School

Flyer for photography class at the Berkeley Adult School, 1993.

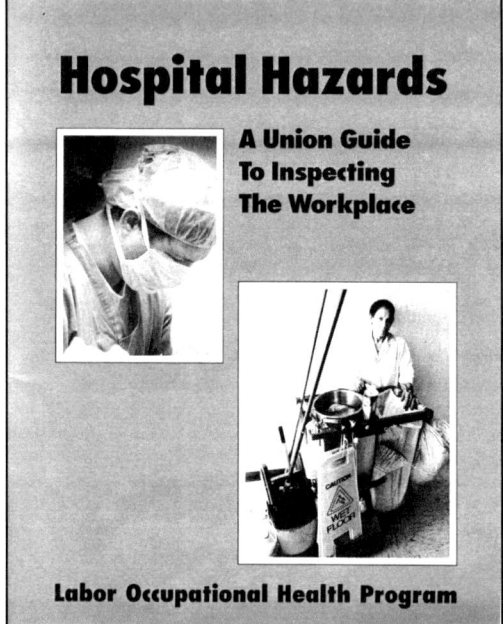

Right: Cover of a promotional brochure for my business, Publishing Solutions.

Examples of publications produced from 1988–2004 for public, private, nonprofit, and academic clients, progressive political campaigns, and individuals. Projects often involved consulting, interviewing, writing, editing, design, and production from start to finish, as in the East Bay Funders community report above. Tom Schultz created the EBF logo. (More examples on page 132.)

RACCOONTEUR

The newsletter for friends of backyard wildlife
Volume I, Number 1 • April 1997

Welcome to RACCOONTEUR—the newsletter for friends of backyard wildlife

RACCOONTEUR is a newsletter devoted to the most curious, intelligent and adaptable wild animal ever to coexist with those strange critters called humans. In these pages we'll inform and entertain you with raccoon stories — not by raccoons personally, but by enthusiastic observers — people who have lost their hearts to these engaging nocturnal visitors.

RACCOONTEUR contains "tails" (furry, ringed and otherwise), anecdotes and information shedding light on the lifestyle of the perennial wild critters that visit our backyards, with or without invitation. We encourage you to send us your own raccoon stories for inclusion in a future issue of RACCOONTEUR. You'll get a byline, and your story will become part of raccoon lore as reported by humans. We recognize that some folks have had less-than-harmonious relationships with backyard critters. Your efforts to coexist with critters who share your turf can help other humans find humane solutions to difficult situations.

So don't "paws"—send your favorite raccoon or other critter story and we'll print it with a byline. (If we need to edit for length, we'll contact you.) Photos are welcome, too. We'll use them if possible and return them in your stamped, self-addressed envelope.

A word to cat and dog lovers: RACCOONTEUR is exclusively devoted to wild animals—those we encounter firsthand in our backyards, our rural and urban neighborhoods, on camping trips—wherever.

Send inquiries and stories to the editor: Marianne Robinson, phone/fax 510-540-0898, or e-mail: pubsol@lanminds.com.

RACCOONTEUR is published periodically with the support of Friends of Backyard Wildlife

Newsletter full of facts and articles by Marianne and volunteer contributors, 1997–2002

CHAPTER SIX
Change and Loss

During the 1980s I managed to visit Amy in Arden a few times, usually during Christmas season. Her tiny, rented cottage reflected the warm, natural aesthetic that was her hallmark. In her living space were books, record albums, her own paintings and photographs, found wood pieces, pottery, plants, old bottles, and simple furniture—all arranged and rearranged to satisfy her artistic taste. And, as in every place she had lived, she transformed her small outdoor space into a one-of-a-kind rustic cottage garden, including a bird bath and bird feeder made by her son Jac. She knew and nurtured each plant, every flower, every stone. She loved to send me color photographs, often made up into tiny booklets, illustrating what she had done with her house and garden. Making the space around her beautiful was an ongoing labor of love.

little stones

she must have found them in the woods
and streams near the places she lived
found each one as she found four-leaf clovers
   said "I find one
   and it gives me the good luck
   to find another"
picked up each stone
each round stone
each oval or flat stone
this one smooth, this one rough
   all of them small—
   they had to be small—
and turned them over in the
palm of her hand

   each one as familiar
      as each old bottle in the window
      the spidery driftwood found long ago
      the pewter plate, bent with age
   each stone
      chosen for its smallness
      its roundness
      its smooth worn-ness
      or its roughness
         like her hands
              after working in the garden

On our visits I would sit facing her on a bench at her pine table under the lamp glow while she shared her latest creative projects, or letters and pictures she had saved to show me. I did not talk much about what I was doing because my life and work were foreign to her. She was so happy just to have me there with her that all else paled by comparison. Her husband Cookie had died in 1975, and her grandchildren and daughter lived far away. Though she had friends nearby, she relied primarily on Jac, who lived 60 miles from Arden.

In her 80s she had a bad fall down her front steps that seriously injured her knee and required home care. When Jac phoned to tell me about her condition, I went to Arden to be with her for a few days, staying with a young woman who kindly offered me a room. I saw how minimally Amy was living, and how difficult any kind of dependency was for her. Meals-on-wheels and help with body functions were tolerated only as long as there was no alternative. Friends who had visited her were concerned. But Amy had her strong opinions, her pride, and limited stamina, which discouraged people from visiting more often. Under pressure to return to work and deadlines, I could stay only five days, but before I left, I made sure she had emergency contact numbers and other resources where she could easily access them.

As that crisis subsided, we wrote back and forth as always, and at one point she asked me to help her "make a little book" of her favorite clippings and writings, many by Mark Twain. She mailed a few things at a time, and with my computer and software, I was able to format and put together a draft of the booklet to show her. But she had visualized something different and said she would send me her book of Mark Twain quotations so I could see what she wanted her book to look like. We worked back and forth for awhile as I mailed drafts to her and received her mark-ups in return. I was happy to help my mother with a meaningful project from the other side of the country.

In March 1994, Jac called to tell me that Amy had had a kidney-related crisis and was recuperating in a nursing facility. He met me at the airport and we went directly to see her. It was painful to witness how miserable she was in a situation in which she felt powerless. She could barely manage a smile, and it was hard to know what to say in the face of her misery. I stayed with the same friend, and the next day Jac told me she had fallen out of bed during the night and was back in the hospital. When I arrived, she was on a gurney outside the emergency room, weak and bruised from the fall and the injections they had administered. She had always been thin, but now she looked like a skeleton. My heartache on seeing my mother in this helpless condition was outdone only by her own pain and suffering. She was moved to a semi-private room on another floor, and when Jac arrived, we stayed with her as long as we could.

As difficult as it was, we faced the probability that Amy would not return from the hospital or nursing home. I walked sadly around Arden, the village where I had grown up, the home Amy would never see again. Jac and I went through some of her carefully saved possessions, and I took some small things that I could carry on the plane—a painting, a few photographs and other mementos, and the "Jackie and Jolly Book" she had made when we were children. Back in Berkeley, I waited anxiously to hear from Jac. In less than a month, word came that she had fallen trying to get out of bed in the hospital. She died in that room, with her beloved son there to ease her passage. He reminded her of what she had told him as a child when he asked what happened to people when they died. "It's like going on a long journey," she had assured her little boy. He sent me the sketch he had made at her bedside after our mother had departed on her journey. She had lived 89 years.

Saying goodbye

This morning I walked the roads of Arden
> water from melting snow, treacherous patches of ice
> cardinals, crows, jays calling from tops of bare gray trees
> chickadees and woodpeckers less raucous...

Amy knew them all.
Here's where she lived for ten years
> transforming the rented cottage and grounds
> into a living, breathing expression of herself...

Here's where I lived as an infant
>	(in an old photo she cradles me in her arms as my father looks on)...
In this house I stole a nickel from Aunt Fan's purse
>	and received a lecture about honesty...
>		(strangers come out of the house with their kids
>		I tell them my aunt lived there and my mother is in the hospital
>		they are kind and friendly)
In this big house I spent eight years as a child and teenager...
>	apple trees in the front yard
>	Victory garden with corn and tomatoes
>	rows of purple iris along the walk
>	cats and kittens on the front porch
>	playing with our dog "Funny"
>		(Amy punishes him if he barks or chases cars)
Behind the big house is the cottage Uncle Lloyd built for my grandparents
>	Eddie died in that house
>	Cora lived there until she was 89,
>	her last year with Amy when she could no longer live alone
>		(in her dementia said "I never had a daughter...")
Walking through the woods
>	leaves crushed into a carpet of ice and mud
>	tears flowing
>	mingled with creek waters...
I'm saying goodbye
>	reluctantly
>	heart heavy
>	full of grief and memories
>		(and puzzling blanks)
Here I sat on the big rock in front of the schoolhouse
>	I went to this two-room school in the 5th grade
>	the rock is gone now
>	the schoolhouse has become a craft center
Here's where my first girlfriend lived every summer
>	with her father and her older sister
>		(her mother was in an "insane asylum")
>	they taught me to play card games
>	they always had a box of chocolates
>		(I was crazy about those chocolates)

Here's the Gild Hall full of memories
    scene of dances
    and plays
    and concerts (Richard Dyer-Bennet, Josh White, Pete Seeger)
    and town meetings
    and Saturday night suppers
    I could tell who was in the hall by the cars and bikes outside
        (this morning some people are cleaning up after a party
        they don't know me
        they can't see my childhood
        in the roof beams, the floor, the beckoning doorway)
I can't bear to look at the cottage she lived in
    before she went to the hospital believing
    she would be back to resume her life
    the cherished birdfeeder Jac made beside the house
    where she could keep an eye on her large bird family
    the little "secret garden" she cleared out of brambles and weeds
    transformed into a place of her own by this woman
My mother
    who had a lifelong knack
    of making the best of what she had
    which wasn't much
    but became beautiful and unique
    under her artistic hand and eye
        (she used to say "I paint with flowers")
Will I ever come back to Arden?
    it seems so far away from my life in California
    and now there will be no family left here
    in this place
    where three generations spent some of the
    best years of our lives
The gray sky echoes my sadness
    as I remember
        and say goodbye.

❂ ❂ ❂

Bright spots

There were bright spots in the 1990s. Client projects and Fellowship activities challenged me and kept me busy, and Tom exhibited and sold paintings in the Bay Area and in Germany. I took a women's workshop called "Birthing a Project" in which I was urged to produce a one-woman show that would illustrate my multidimensional life with songs, poems, photographs, and stories. Like so many good ideas, that one was put on a back burner in favor of producing an income.

Twice Tom and I traveled across the Sierra Mountains; the first time through Truckee and down into Nevada to visit my cousin Phyllis (Henry's niece) and her husband Frank, who had moved from North Hollywood to a small house in Minden. From Carson Valley the four of us drove up into the high mountains, taking in the pure air and the forested areas with tall pines, lakes, and snow packs that had lasted into the middle of July.

The second Sierra trip, in 1995, took us to a folk festival near Bishop on Route 395. We crossed the Sierras north of Yosemite, with craggy mountains rising all around, rushing rivers, volcanic lakes, and breathtaking vistas from every turn in the winding road. Most of all, the mountain air was exhilarating, and I understood why Heidi had recovered from her illness in the Swiss Alps in the book of my childhood.

Down along Route 395, the temperature was 103° during the day, dropping to 95° at night! We stayed in an air-conditioned hotel in Bishop and enjoyed the small-town atmosphere, but tried to stay out of the noonday sun. The festival was in a large meadow with scant shade, and with no lawn chairs we either sat on the grass or stood in whatever shade we could find. Woody Guthrie's protégé and traveling companion Jack Elliot was one of the performers, with a variety of folk-oriented musicians and groups.

During the three-day festival, we left at midday to find some relief from the heat. Our favorite side trip was to the Bristlecone pines at 10,000 feet, with views of Death Valley and the highest Sierra peaks—and the lower oxygen at that dizzying height. Another trip took us beyond the resort area of Mammoth Lakes to Devil's Post-pile, an amazing columnar formation of volcanic rock that is a visual wonder, a photographer's dream. There were towns I wanted to know better, like Truckee, with the East-West railroad through the middle and the main street and old houses that spoke of another time. I brought back photographs of the trip's highlights.

A year later, we flew to Colorado Springs to visit Tom's mother, brother, sister-in-law and other relatives. From there we drove southwest to Durango to see my cousin Sherry (Amy's niece) and her husband for two days, and returned to the Springs on a different route through the Rocky Mountains and river valleys. The Colorado Rockies and the California-Nevada Sierras acquainted me with the "real West" and its startling contrast to the rolling hills and flat countryside I had grown up with on the East Coast.

The best of times

Bill Good was not only Vicki's loving husband, but also a partner in her music career. He served as her manager, producer, and collaborator on all her musical projects. The professional production studio he built in the basement of their Connecticut house was the center for rehearsals, mixing of tracks for presentation of new songs, and much more. As a musician, Bill helped put together bands for recordings and live appearances as well. And Vicki continued to do studio work, singing TV commercials ("jingles") that provided a steady source of income through the 80s and 90s. Those decades, shared with her husband, were surely the happiest and most fulfilling of her life. Her career took her to Florida and California, Brazil, Italy and Greece and, with Gloria Gaynor and other "Disco Divas," to Australia in a "70s revival" tour. Bill went, too, and the travels were part of their life together. At Christmas or Thanksgiving, Vicki came by herself to visit, giving us a chance to spend that precious time together. While I missed getting to know Bill, I appreciated her solo visits as a special gift to reconnect with my daughter at holiday time.

Vicki sent flowers, clothing items, and gift baskets on Mother's Day, my birthday, Christmas—and always photo albums from her travels and celebrations. We kept in touch by letter, cards, phone, and email. A televised appearance and promotional photos taken in 1995 at the fountain in Central Park (wearing her signature blue boa) were especially meaningful because that was where she had spent so much time hanging out with friends in the 60s.

High hopes and bad news

At one point she wrote excitedly about being pregnant, but sadly it ended with a miscarriage. In early 1996 she had a worrisome blood clot removed from a leg, supposedly related to a fall from a bicycle. But within months she was in the hospital, being tested for more serious problems, and the next thing I knew, she was scheduled for surgery for ovarian cancer that had been discovered late in its development. I made plans to go right away, but the surgery was put off a few days and it was touch-and-go as to when I should fly to New Haven. Bill and his mother were with her during the surgery, and I arrived the following morning.

On checking in at the Howard Johnson Motel in New Haven I learned that they provided a shuttle service to the hospital renowned for cancer surgery and treatment. In an otherwise grim situation, the shuttle drivers, waiters, and other service people I met were a blessing. Bill's mother, Jean Good, met me in the waiting room and filled me in on Vicki's condition. Then she handed me a note Vicki had written to give me. Even in her greatly weakened state, my daughter was directing the show! We laughed. It read:

> "Mom — I love you
> 1) Please keep the music playing!!
> 2) NO VISITORS until I'm lucid & presentable!!!
> 3) Spray face with Evian for soothing hydration
> 4) Don't let my hair get too matted!
> Thanks"

She was in intensive care, hooked up to life-support systems, very weak, but smiling and glad to be alive. Soon she was moved to a private room, where I could spend time with her. I helped with all the little things you do in a hospital room—fetching water, arranging pillows, assisting her to the bathroom, answering the telephone. I visited with hospital staff to learn about ovarian cancer (later determined to be cervical cancer). I stayed at the hotel for five nights. When I had to say farewell and return to California to work, Vicki's courage and positive attitude were the hope I took with me. She asserted bravely, "We're going to get through this, Mom."

Soon after I left, Bill took her home, where he had made their bedroom cheerful and bright for her recovery. Within a year the chemotherapy, combined with Vicki's determination, had done its work and she was declared free of the cancer.

Dry Spell Before Rain

I lay awake in bed and said I've had a dry spell
haven't written a word for a long time
and I wondered where the rain is, it's supposed to rain
and I got up and went to the window to listen for rain
and I heard wind and smelled rain but it hasn't started yet
and maybe this is the metaphor—
the dry spell with no writing—
and the rain is on its way.

Couldn't sleep anyway
too much sleep lately
what with a sore throat and flu
and trying to recover
and reeling from the realization
that my daughter has cancer
and seeing her in the hospital
cut open and stitched up
with tubes and catheters and drip bags and
monitoring devices and
the first walk around the bed
with all the attachments pulling and
tugging at her body
and my heartstrings
yet that girl
weak as she was
as hard to move each body part as it was
wasn't about to give up.

She was fighting for her life
like the champion she's always been
a winner, not a loser, giving her
special gifts wherever she goes
"spreads it around" said her minister
who called to send love from the church.

Her mother did what she could
there in that hospital room—
the myriad little things that add up to caregiving—
fetching ice and a cold cloth and hot tea
and turning up the heat
and answering the phone
and straightening up the tables
and supporting her back with my back
as she sat on the edge of the bed
and fetching a nurse and
closing the curtains and
fussing with the flowers
that filled that little room with
love from their senders.

Change And Loss

And now she's back home, sounding like her old self
cheerful, happy, positive
appreciating her loving husband's efforts
to make the room beautiful
praising the roses her Mom sent
enjoying the gifts that have come back to her—
saying "yes" to life.

The rain is falling.
Now I can go back to sleep.

In a state of post-traumatic stress, I kept on working without realizing how numb I was from the shock of seeing my daughter so close to the brink. On a business trip, I fell as I ran up the moving stairs in a subway station, injuring my knee and forcing me to slow down.

Up the Down Staircase

Running up the down staircase
a metaphor for my life
I run but get nowhere
and the stairs keep coming
relentlessly
no beginning, no end
these moving stairs I'm on
spill out before me like
days and
months and years and
I'm exhausted but the stairs
keep coming
their power unstoppable
their speed regulated by an unseen hand

> A man sees my race to get to the top
> holds out a strong arm
> with a hand on the end of it
> "Here, let me help..."
> I reach for it and in the wink of an eye
> I've sprawled headlong
> the steel edge of the stair

    gouging my knee like iron knuckles
    as it moves down like a robot
    to meet my flesh and bones falling up

        Shoulder bag flies before me
        contents sprawl helter skelter on the landing
        the man helps me up
        hands me the fallen BART card
        asks if I'm hurt
        I look down and see blood
        coming through my trouser leg
        he sees that I'm clearly shaken
        offers his arm
        guides me to the booth
        where two young women
        scramble to find a band-aid
        somehow I get to the rest room
        where I try to stem the flow of blood
        and think clearly through the numbness

            in a daze I find a phone and call Tom
            miraculously he's at the other end
            and he comes for me
            as always, over all the years
            the years that tumble down
            as I climb up
            the moving stairs of my life.

    Later I saw that "Up the Down Staircase" was a counterpart to "I Can't Slow Down," a poem written after Amy's death two years before. Keeping busy is a common response to the death of a loved one, a way of avoiding the grim reality. Writing poems, though little comfort, helped me come to grips with my overwhelming sorrow.

Life and work go on

My work life went on as always—working or looking for work, or both. I joined a support group for relatives of cancer patients. Therapy took on new depth and meaning, and I joined a group focused on grief and loss. Besides taking care of myself, I wanted to give Vicki all my love and support across the miles between us.

In the spring of 1997, I was overcome by "total load syndrome," in which my body became overwhelmed by combined fatigue, chemical sensitivity, weakened immune, nervous, and digestive systems, and more. (I called it "the disease that has no name" or chronic fatigue when friends asked.) I could not tolerate smells, noise, environmental and indoor pollution; the stresses of everyday living. For awhile I wore a mask while driving and even at church in order to survive toxins that went unnoticed by others. I got building inspectors to come and assess the condition of my living quarters. The building management company cooperated over several months to make repairs in flooring and windows. Tom took up old, moldy carpets and painted the bedroom and living area. I got rid of old books, records, and clothing, and cleaned out closets as much as possible. And I conducted endless research to learn what was going on in my body, identify treatments and practitioners that might help, experiment with some, and hope things would improve. A substantial portion of my unsteady income went to alternative health care not covered by Medicare or any insurance plan.

That September, less than a miraculous year after her life-saving surgery, Vicki came to visit, doing her own regimen of supplements, exercise, and spiritual rituals during her visit. She and Tom paid for an air filter for my apartment. She was wholly committed to following the rituals she knew would strengthen her body and mind and keep her healthy. At the end of 1997, I found a doctor who specialized in nutrition and holistic medicine. I began seeing her regularly as we focused on supporting and strengthening compromised body systems.

During that year, to help keep me sane, I created a newsletter called *Raccoonteur* to send to friends and relatives with stories, facts, and lore about the backyard neighbors that had won my heart and stirred my fascination. Relatives and other contacts contributed feature articles about raccoons, skunks, chipmunks, and even bears! The four-page photocopied publication, mailed to a list of relatives and friends, emphasized the need for coexistence with the critters we urban dwellers share space with. I published Raccoonteur at irregular intervals, featuring stories, raccoon facts, anecdotes and illustrations from here and there, and an occasional poem. It was another labor of love.

Back in action

Meanwhile, Vicki was back in her life, with periodic gigs at the Greenwich Village club where, for several years, she had been working out the songs and script that she would later use in her one-woman show. In July 1998 she came to my 70th birthday celebration in Tilden Park, which I had planned for months and insisted she come for. The party was a joyous reunion with her California cousins and friends of hers and mine. We sang songs we had sung together in her childhood and teens, cousin Coby played his guitar, everybody sang, Tom presided over the grill, and Teri decorated one of her famous birthday cakes with a raccoon on top! It was a landmark occasion for us all. Photos show a relaxed, mellow Vicki enjoying the whole afternoon's happy, extended-family gathering. No one could know it would be the last time we would ever see her in California, radiant and grateful to be with her family.

On her return to New York, Vicki plunged headlong into developing, producing, and staging a musical theater production that would be the culmination of her life's work. She had rehearsed much of the material at the Village club, and now, working closely with Bill, she added new songs, narrative, and biographical elements that created a musical theater documentary of her life. Her excitement was palpable; I could feel it across the continent in every phone call and email, and I sent what she asked for in the way of biographical information. The show was called VICKI SUE ROBINSON: BEHIND THE BEAT. It was the most original, ambitious, and fulfilling effort of her career.

BEHIND THE BEAT opened in April 1999, at the Kaufman Theater on 42nd Street off Broadway. I had planned to be in the front row on opening night, but as the day approached I faced the truth: I was still weak from the chronic illness that had improved somewhat but was far from over. After agonizing conflict, I emailed Vicki that I wasn't up to making the trip; it would set me back too far in my slow recovery. With every fiber of my being, I hated to let her down and to miss this milestone in her life and career. But she took it well, at least on the surface, and I know she had more than enough to deal with than worrying about Mom coming to town, where I would stay, whether we'd be able to spend any time together. In her never-failing optimism, she said, "Don't worry, Mom. If it goes well, we'll be bringing it to the West Coast."

The production demanded that she be onstage during the entire evening with no intermission, six days a week, performing 22 songs woven together by the script, illustrating her life in music. Two of my friends who attended opening night sent rave reviews about the show with photos taken at a celebration afterwards. And I received an ecstatic email from the star of the show. Here, though I can hardly bear to read it, is the email I received on the day after the show opened:

> "Mom, this IS my life!
> From: Tweetisue@aol.com
> Date: Mon, 10 May 1999 02:01:38 EDT
> Subject: Mother's & Daughter's Day
> To: pubsol@earthlink.net
>
> *Ohhhh Mom!! It was sooooooo damned wonderful I can't stand it!! Standing ovation, flowers and all!!! Anne Quashen was there, we all went together in the cab to the party at a nearby restaurant. I cried in great deep sobs backstage upon leaving the stage for the second time, with 2 bouquets of flowers in hand, the audience on its feet. Just like in the Movies!! I cried with relief after all the fear and worry about my voice and health, pushing through with blinders on one step at a time in slow motion. Doin' it but in a foggy bit. I cried with gratitude at the love pouring onto that stage from all those people, most of whom I did not even know. I cried with deep emotion and love pent up after playing out my life nite after nite as an actress, this time the feelings let go. I cried with a deep wonderful relief that I am still here on this wonderful planet, able to work my craft with body, mind and spirit. I cried for you, my dear sweet Momma, you who gave me strength and courage and wisdom to keep on a-goin', you who gave me wings as a child to fly with song and inspiration.*
>
> *I do love you mom, and you were definitely here tonight up on that stage and in the audience and in the dressing room where sits the lovely bouquet.*
>
> *Please wait another day or so till I rest my voice from this amazing week and I'll call so we can really talk. I'd like to make a trip out there in late summer if I can, as soon as things slow down.*
>
> *Who knows where this thing will go, but you know, right now I am so damned full I'm overflowing, enjoying the right here and now with no expectations or requests of the universe. Just happy as a clam I am I am...*
>
> *Sleep awaits, oh dear mother...I love what you said about Daddy glowing up there wherever he is, he is with me each night on that stage. Finally got him whenever I want him!! Thank you for keeping him alive and well and loved*

for me as a kid and growing up. That was a very generous and loving and respectful thing to do for your daughter (and her father). I will all ways love you more for that!

Happy Mothers Day Mom...my only one!!!!
Your ever-lovin' me......................!

BEHIND THE BEAT ran for two months. Vicki kept in touch by email, mentioning her fatigue and troubling hoarseness—unsettling, but not surprising for a singer onstage for two hours. After the show closed, she clearly needed time to rest and recover from the intense experience. Doctor's visits had been postponed till the show ended, and when she finally went for a check-up, I began to hear about symptoms that could have serious consequences, given her medical history. First it was bronchitis, and then pneumonia, for which antibiotics were prescribed. But symptoms worsened and grew in complexity, including weakness and difficulty breathing.

That fall, she and Bill vacationed in Greece to get away from it all for a much-needed rest. Vicki sent cards expressing her glowing happiness at being in such a beautiful place with her husband, enjoying the simple pleasures in peace after a year of hard work and high stress. Following their return, periods of silence reflected a new round of tests and increasing efforts to find the "magic bullet" that would stop the cancer from spreading. To augment Western medicine, she worked with a practitioner on altering her diet and nutrition to include foods and herbs and teas to support a severely compromised immune system. She kept hoping to "get out there" for Christmas or New Year's, then it was next month...and in a state of constant anxiety, I kept in touch often with messages of love and support and references to alternative treatments.

Between worrying about Vicki and continuing my client projects, I put together some of my poems and published my first chapbook, called *Spiderwebs & Rainbows*. I sent copies to Vicki and a few friends, and took the book with me to poetry readings. I thought, "If I never publish anything else, I'll have this to show for 35 years of writing poems." I also signed up for a course in nutrition with Ed Bauman's Institute for Educational Therapy with the goal of finding a more reliable profession than freelance editing and publishing.

In January Tom's truck was broken into at the bayfront and my handbag was stolen with all my ID, credit card, and keys to my apartment. By notifying the national credit companies immediately, little harm was done, but it was my first experience with identity theft and its potential damage. In February, on a Sunday drive with Tom (me driving), we were in a highway accident that totaled the car and left me without a way to get around for several weeks, while we tried to sell the car and find another one.

Downhill slope

In early April, Vicki called to say she was having difficulty breathing, that she needed oxygen, and she would be going into the hospital in Norwalk. The outlook was not good. Tom and I made preparations to leave at once, then the date was postponed and I was in a minute-by-minute state of suspense. A few days later Bill called from the hospital to say that it would be a good time to come. He handed the phone to Vicki, who spoke through an oxygen mask, trying to sound cheerful to keep Mom from worrying too much. Tom and I boarded the first flight we could get from San Francisco and on April 12 went directly from JFK airport to Norwalk Hospital.

The room was overflowing with flowers, gifts, balloons, toys, cards—expressions of love and caring from friends near and far. Vicki reached out to embrace me, and we wept to see each other for the first time since my 70th birthday not two years before. Soon she was laughing as she pointed to my blue jeans and yellow socks, and said to the friend who was visiting, "Isn't she cute?"

Tom and I visited on Thursday, and on Friday we were at the bedside for a conference with the lung specialist, who advised Vicki that she should remain in the hospital to receive the benefits of oxygen and the observation he could provide there. But Vicki was adamant that she wanted to return to their home, where Bill had arranged to set up portable oxygen tanks and supplies in the room he had fixed up on the ground floor. The next day Bill took charge of getting Vicki settled in her cheerful room with trees and birds outside the window, her comforting photos and familiar objects nearby, and a bathroom next door for easy access.

On Saturday, April 16, filled with sadness and foreboding, Tom and I drove north through Connecticut into New York State while Vicki was being brought home from the hospital. The road took us through a park with a waterfall, where my tears flowed uncontrollably with the tumbling river, grief settling over me like a thundercloud about to burst. The road went past Camp Unity, where I had worked in so long ago in the summer of 1952. It passed through

Sharon and Amenia, small towns where Amy had lived in the 60s and 70s. On the way back to Wilton through Danville and other Connecticut towns, I saw through the fog of foreboding what lay ahead.

On Sunday, relatives and friends gathered informally in the front yard while Vicki lay propped on cushions on a wicker couch, savoring the spring air and the budding trees. Her therapist of 15 years came with her husband. Bill's father, mother and sister came, too, whom we had seen only once since Vicki's wedding 11 years before. Vicki had done what no one in my family had ever thought of—she had asked her family and close friends to be with her in the premature ebbing of her young life. Later the therapist's husband, who had been through a life crisis of his own, lay beside Vicki on her wide bed in silent meditation after words of comfort and solace.

Others, including her mother, lay with her and shared stories or memories as Vicki listened, smiling in uncharacteristic silence behind the oxygen mask. She would jot things down on a note pad or point to something she needed, but her overburdened lungs would not permit the spontaneous words and laughter that lurked behind the mask. But she brightened visibly and moved to the music when Bill played a song she had written and recorded not long before. To me it was the most beautiful song I'd ever heard her sing and, though Bill promised to send me a copy, it never arrived. Its name was "Close Your Eyes."

We returned on Monday, Tuesday, and Wednesday, bringing food or beverages, a back pillow, flowers to brighten the room. On Thursday, when Vicki was scheduled for more tests at the hospital, she asked me to help her bathe before the visit. It was heartbreaking to see how wasted her body had become in the months after the show had closed. She sat on a stool under the shower as I helped her to bathe, dry, and dress quickly so she could return to the oxygen supply.

Vicki had referred us to the woman in charge of groups for relatives of cancer patients, and we attended one gathering, hearing stories from children, siblings, and spouses of patients. I don't recall another person whose child was dying. As Bill wheeled Vicki into the cancer wing in a chair, she clung to my hand and closed her eyes as a nurse gave her a needle in the arm. They then took her to a bed where she was given some intravenous fluid. While she was being tested and treated, I asked to talk directly to the oncologist in charge. When I insisted on hearing the truth of her situation, he said there were still some treatments they could try, but that the cancer had spread to her lungs, and her organs and systems were severely compromised. The prognosis, he said, was "weeks to a year."

Bill took her back home, where she could barely walk with his help from the car to the house and her bedroom haven. Our return flight had been booked for Saturday, April 22, and we tried to be as upbeat as possible as we said our farewells. Everything had been stressful and difficult to bear, but saying goodbye was the toughest challenge of all. As I stumbled for words, Vicki pulled back the oxygen mask and pointed to her mouth. I kissed my beautiful girl on the lips and forced myself to leave the room. It was the last time we ever saw each other.

Back in Berkeley, we were still trying to find a car to replace the one that had been totaled, and daily we drove from one used car lot to another following ads and leads, needing anything that could keep us distracted from obsessing about Vicki's failing strength. Six days after we had returned from Connecticut, I arrived home to find several messages from Bill's mother. Fearing the worst, I called and heard her say, "Vicki is with the angels. She drew her last breath at 8:30 this morning."

No matter how many years later, trying to write anything about that time is nearly as hard as it was to live through the days, weeks, months that followed. Bill Good, functioning on automatic pilot, managed to pull together a memorial service for May 3, just one week after Vicki had died. Tom and I flew back to Connecticut and stayed with Vicki's longtime, gracious friends Kim and Michael Slimak in Westport. The "celebration of her life" was held in the Unitarian church that Vicki had joined some years before. The lovely sanctuary, surrounded by tall trees visible through the floor-to ceiling windows, was filled with flowers, pictures, and costumes characteristic of Vicki's lively stage presence. Family members and friends came who had known Vicki from her childhood and school years; many others had worked with her in the music world; still others knew her from AA (she had just celebrated 15 years of sobriety) and related programs in which she had become a sponsor and mentor.

Bill had asked people close to Vicki to speak, and I felt deeply hurt that I was not included. Someone said he had wanted to keep the ceremony upbeat and minimize tears and emotional outbursts. But I was not about to be left out of my daughter's memorial service. Letting him know my intention, I read a poem I had written years earlier, with introductory remarks about Bill Robinson—the only mention of Vicki's father among all the memories of her life. Bill's relatives were grateful, and I hope others gained greater insight into Vicki's life.

Keeper of the Flame

Vicki Sue—
        child of Bill and Jolly
        child of love and dreams and fire
        keeper of the flame
out of the cauldron
of your parents' love
        of humanity
        freedom
        justice
        equality
        and the simple joys of life on earth
expressed in our lives
        our art
        our politics
you emerged—
        sassy, sweet
        vulnerable, tough
        loving, laughing
        longing, sad—
                whole.

From the seething furnace of our flesh and spirit
        our searching and stumbling
        victories and defeats
you have forged a new amalgam
tested your steel and
found it durable and strong.

Your native gifts—
        strength
        resiliency
        generosity
        compassion
        music
        the audacity to be yourself
        and the courage to get help—
have guided you
        through threatening storms

>   past dizzying whirlpools
>   to a safer, calmer harbor.
>
> Vicki Sue—
>   your life
>   and your art
> are about love
>   friendship
>   trust
>   and sharing
> your politics are
>   recovery
>   growth
>   healing
>   and peacemaking—
> all needed desperately
>   by this race we call human
>   on this planet we call home.
>
> Vicki Sue—
>   daughter of Bill and Jolly—
> you have caught the flaming torch.
>
> Bear it proudly
>   hold it high
>   and keep it burning brightly.

Somehow I survived the nightmarish return flight in a state of unbearable exhaustion, holding myself together for the trip. The world looked completely foreign from my back door, my bedroom window. No! NO!! was the overpowering outcry, through rivers of tears and incoherent sounds, as I was forced to face the reality that I would never, ever see Vicki again. Her death had come 45 years and 11 months after the day she was born.

I walked in a daze, grateful that I had daily tasks to keep me going. We found a new used car. I continued working in the here-today, gone-tomorrow mode of self-employed client projects. I participated in two grief and loss support groups over the next six months. It was weeks before I could write anything at all, and then only disjointed words. The first poems came in August, and after that, the only poems I could write were about my beloved daughter, the memories, the pain, the loss of my one and only child.

Waterfront watch

We walked here together
around this waterfront park
she loved the vistas of the Golden Gate Bridge
San Francisco skyline
Marin headlands over there...

Sometimes she jogged ahead, saying
"I'll meet you on the other side"
      (was this a prophesy?)
we took snapshots of each other
she in her jogging outfit
band around forehead
leaning, hands on knees, or
one leg stretched out behind
the picture of health and fitness...

The last time was July 1998
not two years after the cancer surgery
      (I measure everything in years now)
she came for my 70th birthday celebration
stayed at the Marriott over there
hung her stage costumes in the closet
the blue boa, the sequined dress
for an LA gig after our visit
unpacked the herbs and supplements
meditations and readings for healing rituals...

The night before the big picnic in Tilden Park
we had dinner together at the Marriott
watched Fourth of July fireworks from her balcony
never dreaming it would be her last visit...
> *now gulls wheel overhead*
> *cormorants skim the water*
> *coots sail in convoys*
> *the great blue heron*
> *stands statuesque on the meadow*
> *the burrowing owl's wise round eyes*
> *fix me in its unblinking gaze*

She was excited about seeing the owl
on her next visit
which was supposed to be around New Year's
and then later, in January
then maybe February...
In March the fateful phone call
      (I taped it then, but I can't bear to hear it)
"I'm going to get through this, and
then I'll come out, and we'll have the best visit ever..."
still the optimist, fighting against the odds
for an extension of her life...

And within days I was at her hospital bed
in Norwalk, where we broke into tears
as we embraced and kissed through an oxygen mask
the room filled to overflowing with flowers and
cards and gifts from friends and relations
the profusion symbolic of her life of giving
and sharing and bringing joy and support to others...

And then Bill took her home to their house
where he had prepared a downstairs room
with view of birdhouse and
budding trees outside the window
and she held forth there
breathing through the mask
scribbling messages on a pad
smiling and holding my hand as I
lay beside her on the bed...

The prognosis, said the doctor,
was "weeks to a year..."

As I left her bedside to catch a plane
back to California
she pointed to her lips
pulled the mask back
so I could kiss her on the lips...

It was the saddest parting of 46 years—
and the last.

I walk slowly around the path, weeping
talking to myself about Vicki
our life together, my life now.
> *the burrowing owl has disappeared*
> *a pelican flies overhead*
> *ground squirrels dart here and there*
> *sparrows chitter over a new nest*
> *the resident blue heron flaps low*
> *and lands on a grassy slope.*

Vicki, my daughter,
I wanted to take this walk with you,
but you have departed on a longer journey
leaving me on this path, alone.

Amy at her kitchen table in 1975.

Below: Sitting between her son and daughter, 15 years later

Tom and Marianne on a day trip up the Northern California Coast.

Marianne at Point Reyes during her years as a "red-head."

Vicki shown here on a trip to Florida with Bill in the early 90s . . .

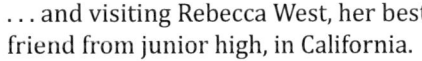
. . . and visiting Rebecca West, her best friend from junior high, in California.

For my 70th birthday in July 1998 I reserved a picnic area in Berkeley's Tilden Park and invited friends and relatives. We all sang together, sitting on picnic tables. That's Vicki clapping, flanked by her cousin Coby Smolens and her Mom on guitar.

On her return to Connecticut, she and Bill put all their efforts into creating and producing "Behind the Beat," a one-woman show with band and back-up singers that opened at the Kaufman Theater in the spring of 1999 (see next page).

Above (L-R): Program for "Behind the Beat" at the Kaufman Theater in New York, 1999.

People Magazine (January 1, 2001) carried this full-page color photo in its Tributes to notable people who died in 2000. Singer KC of the Sunshine Band said, "She was a very strong person. When you stood around her, she exuded so much energy and so much life. You could tell she had a good heart—I never saw her get upset with anyone. She was always ready to go, and she made you feel good before a show. There was an aura around her."

CHAPTER SEVEN
Into the 21ˢᵗ Century

The biggest question that haunted me after Vicki's death was: "Why am I still here when my daughter is gone?" One wise person mused, on hearing of my loss, "Life is such a mystery." Another found a metaphor in astronomy: "They say the brightest stars burn out the fastest." Those comments were more comforting than all the rest put together, all the lame and worn-out phrases like "I can't imagine what it's like to lose a child" or "No one should have to outlive their child." How about a hug and a heartfelt "I'm so sorry for your loss"? I discovered, up close and personal, that the most well-meaning people in our culture are unprepared to deal with death. Even to say someone "died" is avoided like the plague, while "passed away" is acceptable. The death of an adult child gets little attention in the literature, the support groups, the professionals trained to deal with death and dying, grief and loss.

Somehow I lived through each day, put one foot in front of the other. I wept unstoppable rivers of tears at night, or while driving over familiar streets, walking at the waterfront, sitting on a bench in the neighborhood, or at Sunday services. Hearing music from the 60s and 70s triggered tears no matter where I was—especially songs we sang together, and listening to her records was impossible. It took a long time to internalize words like "Vicki would want you to get on with your life" or "she would want you to be happy" or ". . . but you have your memories." Memories, yes—and the hard times as well as the happy times of 46 years were painful to recall because they were all I had left. All I knew was that Vicki wanted, to her last breath, to be here, to live the rest of her life. When I could write at all, poems helped me to grieve, to express my sorrow and love, to recall Vicki's life, her indomitable spirit and strength and love. After a time, when I was publishing a book of poems or reading to an audience, or singing a song, or showing my photographs, I began to feel her presence, to hear her saying, "Go for it, Mom!"

Bill Good had managed all the personal and legal details that followed her death as he had done in the years after her cancer surgery, and we communicated by email at first. He promised to send a videotape of the off-Broadway show, the unrecorded song "Close Your Eyes," and an album of childhood photos I had made for her, but they never came. I kept sending cards and emails in compassion and grief in the hope that he would answer, but I never heard from Vicki's husband again.

Keeping busy

Editing a book on nutritional healing for a health educator helped to keep me going that first year. As a trade for nutrition classes it paid no cash, but other work was slow, and I needed something to keep my grief at bay. Tom and I produced an outdoor exhibit of my New York photographs and his paintings at the Fig Tree Gallery in Berkeley. And I continued attempts to get grandfather Ozer Smolenskin's book, *Geklibene lider,* published in 1933, translated from Yiddish to English. I tried to find a journal that would publish the introduction, a brief history of his life in his words, with a few of his poems. After reading a translation of his first-person story, and fearing his life journey might never be known, I had written a long poem, "I am your granddaughter," about the legacy I inherited from my rabbinical student-turned-radical anarchist grandfather.

With no paid work on the horizon, I contacted Studs Terkel, who referred me to Les Orear of the Amalgamated Meat Cutters about publishing the 1949 Union Caravan story. Orear referred me to two university professors from the Midwest, with whom I collaborated on an article that was published in the Winter 2000/2001 issue of *Labor's Heritage Magazine.* "They Came to the Fair" documented the period of Midwest labor history in which the UPWA (Packinghouse Workers) Caravan had played a significant role in the summer of 1949. One of the most satisfying and affirming projects ever was seeing a seminal experience in my life and the history of the labor movement in print, and in labor archives. As with so many other meaningful projects, the published article was a "labor of love."

The next year a major personal project, between newsletter deadlines, was producing and publishing a second book of poetry titled *Pieces Together.* I chose a larger, square-backed format with a black-and-white Tom Schultz drawing on the cover and found a small press to do the printing. With partial funding given by two Fellowship members, 200 copies were printed, and Tom and I distributed books to independent bookstores in the Bay Area from Hayward to Guerneville. We would drive to small towns, visit the local bookstore, and leave a couple of copies on consignment. Several Berkeley and Oakland stores took it and agreed to the usual 60/40 percentage of the $12 price for each issue sold. Not a lucrative enterprise, but satisfying to know that my poetry book was out there. Poets may become well-known, but rarely wealthy. Most fulfilling was being featured at readings at bookstores and poetry venues, in which having a new book always helps.

New client projects

In 2002, I received a call from an editor I knew asking if I wanted to take over her newsletter work for clients. Barbara had been fighting cancer in the form of a brain tumor and was losing her ability to write or speak coherently. As with a gifted musician who could no longer hear, or a painter whose sight was nearly gone, this was a cruel blow. It took all the patience we could muster to communicate about the details of her projects, but we persevered. I contracted with three of her clients to take over their newsletters, each on a different publishing schedule, and agreed to pay Barbara a finder's fee. She died less than a year after that. Two of those projects lasted about a year before being given to someone who did a less professional job for less money. The best-paid and most interesting newsletter involved writing articles based on my interviews with medical and dental professionals, either onsite or by phone with a tape recorder. I then transcribed the interviews and had them approved by each interviewee while designing, editing and producing the quarterly publication.

That year I initiated, produced, and hosted the Fellowship Café & Open Mike, a monthly Friday night series held in Fellowship Hall for poets and storytellers, songwriters and musicians. As part of Fellowship outreach to the community, the Board agreed to budget a small amount for expenses over and above what was taken in at the door. I booked a featured artist for each event and publicized it widely in the media and by posting flyers in public places. A crew of volunteers handled the many tasks to be done on the night of the Café. For three and a half years the Café succeeded in attracting and showcasing performing artists from the Bay Area. Among featured artists were poets Piri Thomas, Jack Hirschman, Floyd Salas and many more; pianist Mary Watkins; drummer Owen Davis; singer/musicians Country Joe McDonald, Francisco Herrera, Rafael Manriquez, and Alan Smithline; storyteller Nancy Schimmel; and folksingers Faith Petric, Maxina Ventura, and Hali Hammer.

Every month I continued to edit and produce *The Communicator,* the newsletter distributed to Fellowship members, friends, and visitors. Between monthly deadlines I compiled and published two more chapbooks: *Becoming Is All,* poems and prose written in New York, 1964-79; and *Awake at 2 A.M.,* more poems from my collection. I took these four books with me to readings and sold or gave them to friends and relatives.

In late 2002, my doctor referred me to the cardiology department at Alta Bates Hospital for tests related to chest pain, weakness, and other symptoms. The tests showed that I had an irregular heartbeat that might warrant a Pacemaker if it got worse. He told me to come back in a year. Four months later, in February 2003, after marching in a huge anti-war demonstration in San Francisco protesting the imminent invasion of Iraq, I awoke in the middle of the night sweating and unable to breathe. I could not find a pulse. Tom came immediately, called an ambulance and within an hour I was headed for the hospital. They said it was heart block. Twelve hours later, a Pacemaker was implanted in my chest, and the next day I went home with a titanium, battery-powered device regulating the flow of blood through the heart chambers.

One day I received a phone call from Michael Guenon, a young man who lived in Fresno. He explained that he was a cousin several times removed and had been researching the Potter family history. He had gotten my name and whereabouts from my cousin Sherry Potter Walker, Uncle Lloyd's daughter. Sherry had interviewed many relatives some years before and had constructed a family tree. Michael and I began sharing family stories by email, and that summer, on vacation from teaching public school, he came to visit with his wife Linda. He told me about two other cousins of his generation who also lived in California.

While I was getting accustomed to the strange device dwelling in my chest, I produced a Sunday program to celebrate my 75th birthday at the Fellowship. "People's Songs—A Living Tradition" centered around my early experiences with singing in labor and progressive movements of the 1940s and 50s, before the "folk song revival" of the 60s. In the script were songs from the 1948 Progressive Party campaign, the Union Caravan tours, and the Cold War/McCarthy era. Eliot Kenin accompanied me and held forth with "Talking Atomic Blues," Nancy Schimmel sang with me on "The Same Merry-Go-Round," and the congregation joined in singing all the songs in the spirit of the occasion. Jim Hart, a cousin Michael Guenon had told me about, showed up with his wife from Santa Barbara, and my nephew Coby Smolens came from Marin County. It was a joyous celebration. But I was painfully aware of the absence of my one and only Vicki Sue, who would have sung harmonies and swapped verses with me as she had done five years earlier at my 70th birthday party in the park and on two earlier occasions at the Fellowship, not to mention the sweet years of her childhood in Philadelphia and New York.

I had been seeking someone who would work with me on recording an oral history to sort out and document the chronology of my life. Since I was not famous and my multidimensional life did not fit a funding category, I discovered I was not eligible for grants issued by university libraries or grant-making institutions. After pursuing several referrals, in early 2004 I decided to work with Cathy Cade, a personal historian and photographer. We worked out an agreement and schedule for interviews in my apartment twice a month for four months. When it was over, I had 14 audiotapes to be transcribed. They remained in a box on a shelf for the rest of that year, during which I turned 76.

That May I put together a fifth book of poems, *Yesterday and Today*. With a few new poems, it was intended to represent the "best of" my work that I could take to readings.

In October after much back-and-forth for several months, the prestigious West Coast building management corporation "made other arrangements" to publish the newsletter I had produced and edited for two years. When I asked for full payment of the money due me under our revised contract, they offered part-payment only. After a laborious process of negotiating with the higher-ups, a lawyer I consulted with advised me to take them to Small Claims Court. I served notice to that effect, and at the 11th hour, rather than go to court over such a small sum (for them), a staff member notified me that the check for $4000 was in the mail. Case closed.

Retirement?

After 17 years of self-employment, I made the big decision to "retire myself" as of January 2005. This was a radical idea spurred by the loss of the last client, chronic fatigue, and the need to slow down, and it felt scary and unreal. I would try to live on Social Security, the small stipend for the Fellowship newsletter, and Tom's contributions. I would work on my autobiography and other personal projects too long on the back burner. I would give up producing and hosting the monthly Café & Open Mike and keep my volunteer commitments to a minimum. The monthly newsletter would keep me plugged into the Fellowship community, along with periodic participation in Sunday programs and group email lists.

No sooner had I made a good start on transcribing my taped history than I agreed to be part of a Task Force to prepare the ground for a qualified professional to lead the congregation in ways that had been recommended by the Pastoral Consultant and the Elders Group the year before. After five months of research and meetings, amid much skepticism and disagreement among congregants, a special congregational meeting approved the formation of a Search Committee to find a half-time Consulting Minister within the Unitarian Universalist Association (UUA) network. I agreed to chair the seven-member committee, and for another three months of intense communication and meetings culminating in interviews with applicants the committee selected a candidate for approval by the Board of Trustees. Finally, the Board voted unanimously to hire the first professional with "minister" in his/her title in 11 years.

At his first sermon with the Fellowship, my introduction to Rev. Kurt Kuhwald began:

> "When I came to this Fellowship in 1987, I was seeking a community of kindred souls with values akin to those of the village where I spent my formative years. As a lifelong atheist and political activist, I could not have foreseen that I would be part of a search for a minister in a church of any kind! But my life journey has taught me that there is a universal human need for community that can give meaning, comfort, inspiration, and sustenance in ways that are not found in other institutions or relationships."

In January 2007 Eliot Kenin and I teamed up to lead a Woody Guthrie Songs workshop at the Annual Western Workers Festival. We got everybody singing Woody's songs in the true spirit of People's Songs Hootenannies. At a poetry workshop there, I met Tiny (Lisa Gray-Garcia), a poet, activist, and founder of Poor News Network, and invited her to present a Sunday service at the Fellowship.

That spring I put together a sixth book, *Poems for Vicki,* of poems I'd written during and after the last 15 years of her life. The cover photograph is from a series I made of her at 19 in Manhattan during the year before "Turn the Beat Around" was recorded and became world-famous.

For some years, chronic fatigue and related conditions had been minimizing my capacity to enjoy activities I once took for granted. When people said, "You look good!" I was often surprised, as it was not how I was feeling. From 2007 forward, I experienced a series of physical setbacks that increased the stress. I was being forced to simplify my life, slow down, get more rest and reduce the stress load. These had never been my strong suit, but necessity was taking over. I stopped coloring my hair after 15 years of being a "redhead." I cut off high-priced cable TV and gave away the heavy old television that took up space and blocked light in the living room. That felt liberating. After 16 years, I resigned as newsletter editor for the Fellowship. I began giving away personal household items, records, books, photos, and other mementos to relatives.

An ongoing project that kept me busy was preparing the "materials of my life"—all the documents, publications, photographs, "stuff" stored in boxes, file cabinets, closets, on shelves and walls—to send to two archival collections that welcomed them. Another was the challenge of finding a publisher for my autobiography, finishing the years-long work of writing and revising the book, and seeing it in print.

Program cover for a Sunday service at the UU Fellowship celebrating People's Songs and singing as activism on my 75th birthday, July 2003. The photo of Pete Seeger with Henry Wallace on tour is from the *People's Songs Bulletin,* September 1948, during the Progressive Party campaign.

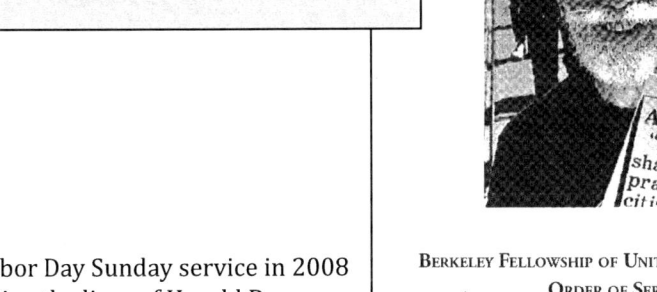

A Labor Day Sunday service in 2008 honoring the lives of Harold Rossman and Martha Roberts, devoted long-time members and leaders of the Berkeley UU Fellowship.

With Tom at one of many anti-war protests in San Francisco during the build-up to the invasion of Iraq in 2002-03.

Below: Part of an outdoor exhibit of Marianne's photographs and Tom's paintings at the Fig Tree Gallery, Berkeley, 2002.

Above: A flyer for the Fellowship Café & Open Mike produced monthly from 2002-2005. (Graphic by Rodney Dunican)

Epilogue

Life continues to unfold day by day. I have trouble believing I'm the same person I once was, but I have learned to live with the person I am now. I am eternally grateful for Social Security and Medicare, programs that working people pushed for and won. Any financial assets I may have had are long gone, used to supplement erratic income that was rarely the same from one year to the next.

Tom's help and caring and loyal support is beyond measure. After 41 years of separate finances and different priorities, we are still "significant others," partners, companions. We see each other nearly every day, go for walks, talk on the phone. He needs his live-and-work studio for both fine art painting and carpentry work, and I could never have done my professional work and personal projects without a computer and office set-up. We've had our disagreements and difficult times—and we never fail to rebound out of mutual love, shared experience—and longevity.

And now, after many revisions to this last chapter, I must arrive at a stopping place. How shall I end the story? Only time can tell. Maybe life is a never-ending journey, a cycle, a mystery. I prefer to leave it as I have lived it—with more questions than answers.